How we won
The Ashes

How we won
The Ashes

Foreword by TOM GRAVENEY

Methuen

Content, editing and design by
PA Sport
Bridgegate
Howden
DN14 7AE
www.pa-sport.com

PA Sport Leading the world in sports information

Ashes Urn image courtesy of MCC
Pictures: PA, Empics & The Gloucester Echo

Published by Methuen 2005
First published in 2005 by
Methuen Publishing Limited
11-12 Buckingham Gate
London
SW1E 6LB

Printed and bound in Great Britain by
Bookmarque Ltd, Croydon Surrey

Contents

Foreword by **Tom Graveney**, President of MCC, 2004–05   1

Ashes History   2

Five great Ashes battles   2

2004 – England's golden year   6

England in the mood   10

First Test, Lord's   12

Man of the Match, Glenn McGrath   34

Second Test, Edgbaston   37

Reaction   56

Man of the Match, Andrew Flintoff   58

Famous close Tests   60

Third Test, Old Trafford   62

Man of the Match, Ricky Ponting   86

Fourth Test, Trent Bridge   87

Man of the Match, Andrew Flintoff   108

Fifth Test, The Oval   109

Man of the Match, Kevin Pietersen   137

Players of the Series   138

Celebration time   141

What they said   146

England's Series in statistics   150

Australia's Series in statistics   152

All-time records   154

What's next for England   156

Tom Graveney's Test career ran from 1951 to 1969 and he played in 79 Test matches.

Foreword by Tom Graveney

Former England batsman and President of MCC 2004–05

The 2005 Ashes has been one of the most outstanding Test series ever contested. Before a ball had been bowled in the first match at Lord's, the atmosphere on the ground was absolutely electric.

In the early exchanges (of words) the Australians were full of confidence – they said they would win 5-0, that England could not bowl them out twice with their attack, and so on. On the first day, England's bowlers let them know that that wasn't true – three direct hits on the helmet and not much sympathy shown to the tourists put down a marker for the series.

There is no doubt that England had prepared well and that skipper Michael Vaughan and coach Duncan Fletcher had, between them, engendered a tremendous team spirit in the dressing-room and on the field from the first ball. Everyone seemed to know what was expected of them and no time was wasted discussing tactics on the field, unlike the Australians. Mind you, they hadn't been on the wrong end of the stick for a long time!

Perhaps the most satisfying thing, after a couple of minor incidents, was the way the game was played by both sides. There was a feeling of respect for each other.

In any series there are going to be umpiring errors and for the most part these were accepted and forgotten. The players had a smile and a handshake for the opposition and they were a wonderful example for the thousands of children watching. The catalyst for this probably started with the friendship of Shane Warne and Kevin Pietersen, who were team-mates at Hampshire. Then there was Andrew 'Freddie' Flintoff consoling Brett Lee at the end of the Edgbaston match. As Keith Miller always said, 'it's only a game!' This, I'm sure, will lead to friendships that will last forever.

Everyone did their jobs, but two men were absolutely terrific. Warne probably proved he is the greatest leg-spinner of all time – and he can bat too – while Flintoff was a tower of strength in every way: batting, bowling and sportsmanship.

At the end of it all I felt both deserved the Compton-Miller medal for being Man of the Series. Although only Flintoff was given the award, I do not think Keith Miller or Denis Compton would have argued if Warne had received one as well.

Ashes history

It may be the smallest trophy in world sport, but the Ashes urn is one of the most highly coveted and is steeped in history.

The origin of the Ashes dates back to 1882 when Australia recorded their first victory on English soil, prompting the *Sporting Times* to print the following spoof obituary:

'In affectionate remembrance of English cricket which died at the Oval, 29th August, 1882. Deeply lamented by a large circle of sorrowing friends and acquaintances. RIP. NB — The body will be cremated and the ashes taken to Australia,' wrote London journalist Reginald Shirley Brooks on 29 August 1882.

Three weeks after the Oval defeat England, led by the Hon. Ivo Bligh – later Lord Darnley – travelled to Australia and, although they lost the first Test by nine wickets, after victories in the next two it became generally accepted the team had brought back the Ashes.

The early history of the actual Ashes is still something of a mystery as it was long believed the trophy – a small urn presented to Bligh by a group of Melbourne women – contained the ashes of a bail used in the third match in Australia.

However, in 1998, Lord Darnley's 82-year-old daughter-in-law said the contents actually comprised the remains of her mother-in-law's veil, rather than a bail, while other evidence suggests a ball.

After Lord Darnley's death in 1927 the urn was given to MCC where it still resides in the Lord's museum, together with a specially-made red and gold velvet bag.

Five great Ashes battles

Fourth Test, Headingley, 1948 – Australia win by seven wickets

Don Bradman's 'Invincible' team secured the Ashes by completing a remarkable run chase as time ran out in a match England had edged until the final day. England posted 496 with Cyril Washbrook (143) and Bill Edrich (111) reaching three figures and Len Hutton (89) and night-watchman Alec Bedser, with his highest Test score of 79, making significant contributions. Australia slipped to 68 for three in response but the 19-year-old Neil Harvey (112) and Sam Loxton (93) helped them get to within 38 of the total. England appeared to take control as Washbrook (65) and Hutton (57) made their second century opening stand of the game and Denis Compton and Edrich added half-centuries. They declared early on the final day but the Aussies, led by Arthur Morris (182) and the magnificent Bradman (173 not out), wanted the win and they successfully reached their 404-run target with seven wickets and 15 minutes to spare.

Fourth Test, Old Trafford, 1956 – England win by an innings and 170 runs

A match forever remembered for the incredible feats of Jim Laker, who took an unparalleled 19 wickets as England routed Australia by an innings and 170 runs. There was little hint of the sensation to come as Australia's spinners struggled in England's innings. Peter Richardson (104) and Colin Cowdrey (80) put on 174 for the first wicket in just three hours and the Rev. David Sheppard (113) added another century. Australia's reply began in the afternoon session of the second day but they could not handle the combination of a wet wicket and Laker's spin. By the close they were already following on. Rain affected the next two days but Laker finished them off on the final day, recording figures of nine for 37 and 10 for 53.

Third Test, Headingley, 1981 – England win by 18 runs

The 500/1 miracle. Only once had a side ever won a Test after following on and such was England's dire position that a number of players checked out of their hotel on the fourth morning. At that point they were already one wicket down in their second innings and still needed another 221 more to make Australia bat again. Enter a certain Ian Botham, who had endured a miserable first two Tests and resigned as captain prior to Headingley. He made something of a point with 50 in England's poor response to Australia's 401 for nine and by taking six wickets, but that was nothing compared to what followed. He smashed a remarkable 149 not out and shared in a vital 117-run stand with tailender Graham Dilley as England at least posted a target of 130. The odds were still against them, but Bob Willis bowled like a man possessed to take eight for 43 and win the match by 18 runs.

Fourth Test, Melbourne, 1998 – England win by 13 runs

England had seemed down and out after an abject defeat in the third Test and a humbling loss to an Australian second-string side. Yet, cheered on by the Barmy Army, they somehow managed to defy the odds and secure an unexpected morale-boosting victory that briefly brought the series back to life. Captain Alec Stewart hit a century, but Steve Waugh (122 not out) responded with one of his own to give Australia a first-innings lead of 70. Stewart, Nasser Hussain and Graeme Hick scored fifties as England forged back ahead and Alan Mullally added a few lower-order swishes but a target of 175 was still well within the hosts' capabilities. At 103 for two and, later, 140 for four, Australia were well on the way but Kent seamer Dean Headley then delivered the performance of his short career, six for 60 including a spell of four for 4 in 13 balls, as England won by 13 runs.

Waugh had looked set to break English hearts, forcing the extra half an hour on the fourth evening as he tried to close out the game – a decision which, at the time, was disputed by Stewart, who was keen for his bowlers to have a rest and return the following morning. While Headley was performing his heroics, Waugh remained stoutly unbeaten at the far end. However, he took a single to leave Stuart MacGill to face the bowling of Darren Gough, and the Yorkshireman produced two of his finest inswinging yorkers firstly to send MacGill back to the pavilion and then, two balls later, have Glenn McGrath trapped lbw to seal a memorable win for England.

Fourth Test, Headingley, 2001 – England win by six wickets

This time the series had already gone Australia's way. The tourists were superior in all departments and comfortably won the opening three Tests to retain the Ashes.

They were in control at Headingley too, Ricky Ponting (144), Damien Martyn (118) and Glenn McGrath (seven for 76) helping them to a first-innings lead of 138. It could have been a far bigger deficit for England had Alec Stewart, batting at an unusually low number seven, not smashed an impressive unbeaten 76 from just 83 balls, which included 10 fours and a massive six off McGrath. He put on 80 with Mark Ramprakash (40), and then helped England recover from 252 for six to register 309 all out thanks to some impressive stroke-play and good support from the tail.

Ponting (72) again got the second innings off to a good start but with time running out, stand-in skipper Adam Gilchrist – deputising for the injured Steve Waugh – decided to declare, preferring to push for another win rather than settle for a draw.

England had a final-day target of 315 to chase but after losing openers Michael Atherton and Marcus Trescothick to leave the score at 33 for two, it seemed unlikely. It was then that Mark Butcher, who came close to being dropped after a late night out during the previous Test at Trent Bridge, played the innings of his life. He cracked a remarkable 173 not out to lead England home by six wickets. He was ably supported by skipper Hussain (55) in a partnership worth 181, and then Mark Ramprakash (32), but the day was all about Butcher and an innings which Stewart described as his Surrey colleague's 'best ever' which set up England's second highest run chase to beat Australia – beaten only by the 332 chased to win a Test back in 1928/29.

2004 – England's golden year

Expectation has always outpaced reality during the build-up to recent Ashes series as English teams full of talent were primed for the task of reclaiming the famous old urn.

That talent has often come under critical scrutiny over the course of eight fruitless campaigns, although even the Australians have conceded that the ability in their opponent's ranks has never been in question.

England have won individual Tests against their oldest rivals but have not contained enough resolve, or indeed sufficient fit bodies, to provide a sustained challenge since relinquishing their grasp on the historic trophy 16 years ago.

Few will forget the humbling meted out to the Aussies at Edgbaston in 1997 or indeed the nailbiting English victory at Melbourne on the 1998/99 tour when series were still alive.

Other wins, however, have come in dead rubbers when the Australians are perennially susceptible to defeat.

But the evidence that things could be different this time was compelling given the *annus mirabilis* Michael Vaughan's men experienced in 2004.

During the previous year, Vaughan's side dealt brilliantly with every challenge that was placed in front of them; whenever their character was tested, England came through, winning 11 and drawing two of the 13 Test matches they played.

They were the only side in world cricket to remain unbeaten, in fact, and their win ratio exceeded even that of world champions Australia.

England's serious Tests began in the heat of Jamaica, and Steve Harmison began his ascent to the top of the Test bowling rankings.

The date was March 14 when a peaceful Sunday morning was wrecked by Harmison at Sabina Park. Having previously taken his international wickets in dribs and drabs, this haul was in bulk.

Persistently aggressive, he claimed seven wickets for a paltry 12 runs, also having two chances missed along the way.

Whereas previous regimes sought success via containment, England now had a primal form of attack and employed it whenever

Michael Vaughan gets a deserved taste of champagne as England celebrate their 4–0 Test series demolition of West Indies that fuelled the belief they could realistically challenge the Australians

Harmison was fresh, occasionally when he was not and no matter what the situation was.

With Matthew Hoggard, in tandem, swinging the ball prodigiously whenever conditions suited and Andrew Flintoff and Simon Jones also developing the ability to arc the ball through the air, Vaughan's artillery now contained nous as well as needle.

Like his close friend, Harmison, Flintoff increased his productivity as a wicket-taker, registering a maiden five-wicket haul in Barbados.

When the rough 'uns failed to rough up, the reliable Ashley Giles exploited a different kind of rough, adding to the attacking options just weeks after his continued selection as an international spin bowler was called into question.

His major success came against the West Indians at the end of summer 2004 when he finished as England's leading bowler, often inheriting Harmison's mantle as partnership breaker as the fast-bowling spearhead experienced a rare lean spell in mid-season.

Such was the confidence exuded from the 3-0 win in the Caribbean that Giles, who often had been employed merely to block up an end, was able to express himself in a new role.

Winning became such an infectious habit that even individuals who had been struggling emerged as success stories. Giles' transformation was epitomised by his own version of Shane Warne's 'ball of the century', this one not fizzing across the sizeable frame of Mike Gatting but rather scything through the gate of the great Brian Lara.

It was that moment, more than any other, which encapsulated the changing nature of the current England team.

To complement penetration with ball in hand, established contributors with the bat discovered greater consistency: Nasser Hussain bowed out with a Lord's hundred to get the Test summer started, Vaughan rediscovered form with twin tons off the West Indies attack at the same ground and Graham Thorpe chiselled out runs with a regularity that did justice to his ability.

While those seasoned campaigners performed admirably to kick-start a campaign resulting in a rare perfect home record in a Test summer, the irresistible rise of Andrew Strauss maintained the team's momentum into the winter.

From his stunning initiation on his home ground of Lord's, where he struck a debut hundred against New Zealand, through another ton taken off West Indies later in the summer, the runs continued to flow until he reached South Africa, the place of his birth.

By the time he set foot there he had ratcheted up 590 runs in 14 Test innings, but rather than dwell on past achievements, he excelled further, striking three hundreds to single-handedly carry the tourists through a series in which they rarely sparked.

There was enough impetus carried from the summer to set a new English record eighth consecutive Test victory at Port Elizabeth, but standards failed to match those expected of a team on the up.

When runs were required they were delivered from numerous bats and the 13 matches during the calendar year accounted for 20 centuries.

Just as Strauss took over from Hussain, so Robert Key was the beneficiary of Mark Butcher's multitude of misfortunes triggered by a car crash in July.

Peripheral figures like Key, who struck a double-hundred against the Windies at Lord's and guided England home with an unbeaten 93 at Old Trafford, James Anderson and Ian Bell contributed when necessary.

That, above and beyond anything else, was expected to be the crucial factor if England were to put up a serious challenge in the 2005 Ashes.

Good performances in previous battles against Australia have been in splendid isolation rather than in conjunction with similar displays from team-mates and the sum of the parts would need to add up to something of greater value against Ricky Ponting's men in the Tests.

England were enjoying the most successful spell in their history, and they had developed a trend of wresting the advantage from opponents on the third and fourth days of previously well balanced Tests. This was a habit that had to continue.

England in the mood

Confidence among the English was unusually high heading into the series, buoyed by a dramatic tie against Australia in the one-day NatWest Series final and a hammering handed out to the tourists in their inaugural Twenty20 meeting – when the Aussies crashed to an astonishing 100 run-defeat at Hampshire's Rose Bowl.

The talk among the Barmy Army and the press was that Australia had arrived under-prepared and had not found their five-day form quickly enough, although the long run of one-day matches – many played against the host nation – had helped blow away some of the cobwebs.

There was an air of unbridled optimism among the England players which suggested the time was right to change the established order and record their first series victory over Australia in 18 years.

The team possessed a balance and a confidence. A fearlessness, too, much of which stemmed from the fact that Andrew Strauss, Ian Bell, Kevin Pietersen, Andrew Flintoff and Geraint Jones had never faced a ball in an Ashes Test.

Although that suggested a lack of experience, it also meant the core of England's team headed into the series undaunted by the aura of the Aussies.

These Ashes debutants had not tasted defeat. They carried no scars and against the veterans of Australia, many of whose best days, however glorious, were behind them, that was a major plus point.

And England captain Michael Vaughan was confident he was in charge of a side hitting form at the right time, and one with every chance of claiming victory in the latest chapter of the oldest rivalry in world cricket.

'We're looking forward to testing our ability against the best,' said Vaughan, who replaced Nasser Hussain as captain when the 2003 Test series against South Africa started with a draw, prompting Hussain's resignation.

'We want to see how far we have come. I believe we've come a long way.' South African-born batsman Pietersen, set to make his debut in the first Test at Lord's after making a dramatic impact in the one-day game over the winter was, typically, even more upbeat.

'If England play 25 days of their best cricket then there is a chance. The Australians are so good you cannot give them an inch,' he said.

'England cannot afford to let up, and it is a case of making sure you are right on your game every day of the series.'

Former England captains and Ashes winners Graham Gooch and Ian Botham were both full of expectation that Vaughan's side could change the flow of history against Australia, and that the players of today could join Gooch and Botham in Ashes folklore.

'I think England have the best chance since we last won it in 1986/87. Andrew Flintoff is an absolute key because without him as the outstanding all-rounder England are not that well-balanced,' said Gooch.

'Another key player is Steve Harmison. If he bowls well England know they have someone who can take wickets against the best.

'England have to be aggressive; they have to take the fight to the Australians and get under their skin. They have to try to derail the Australians' gameplan.

'Australia are as good as they have ever been; England are better than they have been in recent years.'

Botham concentrated on England's bowling resources and felt the established attack of Flintoff, Harmison, Matthew Hoggard, Simon Jones and Ashley Giles could use their combined experience to great effect.

But he warned that they would have to step up yet another gear from their winter tour of South Africa if they were to taste victory.

'The bowlers will have to hunt as a pack, and England will have to play 20 per cent better than they did in South Africa if they are going to pull it off.'

However, to succeed they would have to overcome the mastery of leg-spinner Shane Warne, not only the greatest spinner to ever play the game but the Test wickets world record-holder after claiming almost 600 scalps during a long and distinguished career.

Warne, who entrenched himself in Ashes history by delivering the 'ball of the century' which dismissed Mike Gatting in the 1993 series, was playing in his last Test series in England and was determined to go out in the same way he had announced himself – with a bang.

He was desperate to get one over his good friend Pietersen, a team-mate in county cricket at Hampshire, and was in no mood to be part of the first Aussie team since 1985 to relinquish the Ashes.

'I think the other teams have to catch up with Australia – we keep winning so we stay confident in our ability,' he said.

'India in India is perhaps the toughest challenge in cricket – but beating England in the Ashes is right up there.

'I have played six series against England, and we have beaten them every time. I am determined I will not start losing to them now.'

And when the war of words had subsided, the subsequent battle on the pitch did not disappoint.

First Test Day One – Morning session

England's highly rated attack produced a stunning display of high-quality bowling to leave Australia reeling after a compelling first morning's play in the Ashes series.

Aiming to start positively and set the tone for the rest of the summer, England quickly thrust aside disappointment at Australia winning the toss and getting first use of the pitch and tore through the world champions' star-studded top order during an exciting first session.

Matthew Hoggard and Steve Harmison, making the most of cloudy overhead conditions, used the new ball effectively to remove opener Matthew Hayden and captain Ricky Ponting before Andrew Flintoff and Simon Jones made further inroads.

At one stage England had taken three wickets for 11 runs in 15 balls before Jones claimed his important second victim to leave Australia, seeking to defend their 16-year hold on the Ashes, struggling on 97 for five at lunch.

England started with five players making their Ashes debuts – Andrew Strauss, Ian Bell, Kevin Pietersen, Flintoff and Geraint Jones – while seamer Jason Gillespie passed a fitness test on his knee problem to take his place in Australia's line-up.

He had only returned to training the previous day, and despite struggling for form throughout the summer's one-day series, was preferred to Michael Kasprowicz as the third seamer behind Glenn McGrath and Brett Lee.

McGrath, the world's top-ranked bowler, began the match looking for just one wicket to become only the fourth player in history to claim 500 Test victims.

England's own top paceman Harmison, much happier on home soil after a disappointing tour to South Africa, set the tone from just the second ball of the day when he rapped Justin Langer on the elbow. From that moment Australia felt the full force of the England bowlers' aggression.

Langer was the most impressive of the Australian batsmen in the morning after overcoming his early blow, which needed several minutes of treatment from physiotherapist Errol Alcott. He dominated a 35-run opening stand which was only broken when Hayden (12 off 25 balls) was bowled by Hoggard in the eighth over, the Yorkshire bowler finding some swing to bring the ball back into the left-hander and clip his off stump.

Ponting, who had scored a century on his last appearance at Lord's during the NatWest Challenge, was not as fluent this time and was dropped off Hoggard, before he had scored, by England debutant Pietersen, who dived unsuccessfully to his left at gully.

The Australia captain failed to recover his composure after he was hit on the helmet by another rising delivery from Harmison which he tried to pull with the score at 49 for one in the 11th over. Ponting was cut on the cheek which again forced a delay while he received treatment and the blow obviously unsettled the batsman as 10 balls later he was out for 9 when he edged the Durham fast bowler to Strauss at second slip.

Having claimed those two early breakthroughs with the new ball, England captain Michael Vaughan then made two successful bowling changes as Australia's top order folded under pressure.

Lancashire all-rounder Flintoff's uncanny knack of making something happen was again evident when he struck with his fourth delivery after being thrown the ball by Vaughan. He tempted Langer (40) into an ill-advised pull shot which flew high in the air and was collected by Harmison at square leg.

England's excitement at Flintoff's breakthrough heightened three balls later when Jones – with his first delivery of the match –

AUSTRALIA: first innings

J L Langer c Harmison b Flintoff	40
M L Hayden b Hoggard	12
R T Ponting c Strauss b Harmison	9
D R Martyn c G O Jones b S P Jones	2
M J Clarke lbw b S P Jones	11
S M Katich not out	7
A C Gilchrist not out	8

Extras b1 w1 nb6 8
Total 5 wkts (23 overs) 97

Fall: 1-35, 2-55, 3-66, 4-66, 5-87.
To Bat: S K Warne, J N Gillespie, G D McGrath.
Bowling: Harmison 7-0-32-1, **Hoggard** 7-0-33-1, **Flintoff** 5-1-16-1, **S Jones** 4-0-15-2.

had Damien Martyn (two) caught behind by Geraint Jones chasing a wide ball, leaving Australia 66 for four.

Jones followed up with the crucial dismissal of Michael Clarke, trapped leg before for 11 in the over before lunch, to give England the best possible start to the series with the tourists reeling at 97 for five.

Day One – Afternoon session

England's aggressive display in the morning session was followed up after lunch with Harmison providing the spearhead for the attack which dismissed Australia for a lowly 190 as the series began in gripping fashion.

Harmison claimed five for 43, including a burst of four for 7 in 14 balls, as Australia's decision to bat first looked to have backfired on them.

Reeling at 97 for five at the interval, Australia's hopes of reaching a competitive total rested with Simon Katich and Adam Gilchrist, and they set about punishing all loose deliveries after lunch.

Gilchrist quickly raced to 26 off 19 balls, which included six boundaries, but he went overboard with his positive approach as Flintoff struck a huge blow with the score on 126.

The Australian wicketkeeper-batsman, who can be such a devastating force once into his stride, went for another ambitious shot and succeeded only in nicking the ball through to Geraint Jones behind the stumps. Flintoff could not contain his delight and cut an excitedly animated figure as he wildly celebrated dismissing a player who has been a thorn in England's side on many occasions.

New batsman Shane Warne looked far from comfortable and was relieved when he edged a rising delivery from Flintoff over the slips to the boundary, but he then produced a more convincing shot in carving the Lancashire all-rounder over point to the ropes.

Warne quickly raced into the 20s and the 150 came up for Australia in only the 32nd over, while at the other end Katich was content to shore up an end with England only one wicket away from breaking into the Australian tail.

The attack from the leg-spinner, a handy lower-order batsman himself, prompted captain Vaughan to recall Harmison with the intention of intimidating Warne – and hopefully the rest of the lower order – with some high-quality fast bowling.

The theory proved valid as, after an entertaining 28 off 29 balls from Warne, who shared a 49-run stand with Katich off only 47 balls,

Harmison removed the spinner's leg stump as he stepped across his wicket.

Katich was bullied into his first rushed shot of a 106-minute innings, pulling a short delivery that flew high in the air and was collected by Geraint Jones after he ran back from his usual wicketkeeping position.

His departure for 27, which included five fours, with the total on 178 for eight, signalled the end for Australia.

Harmison, spurred on by those two quick wickets, continued to charge in and fellow paceman Lee (3) had no answer as he edged behind to give Jones his fourth catch of the innings.

The last-wicket pair of Gillespie and McGrath is not the most solid in world cricket and they added only 12 – the latter making 10 not out in only six balls courtesy of hitting two fours – before the ineffective Gillespie was pinned in front by Harmison.

That wicket gave the Durham fast bowler the sixth five-wicket haul of his Test career and handed England a great opportunity to stamp their authority on the series and claim a significant psychological – and numerical – advantage so early in the summer.

'It is the first time I've got five wickets at Lord's, and it is more special getting it against Australia. I enjoyed the fact a few plans came through for me and I was pleased with the way that I bowled,' said Harmison afterwards.

There were six overs left before tea and openers Marcus Trescothick and Andrew Strauss successfully negotiated the period, reaching 10 without loss at the interval.

AUSTRALIA: first innings
(Continued: 97-5)

J L Langer c Harmison b Flintoff	40
M L Hayden b Hoggard	12
R T Ponting c Strauss b Harmison	9
D R Martyn c G O Jones b S P Jones	2
M J Clarke lbw b S P Jones	11
S M Katich c G O Jones b Harmison	27
A C Gilchrist c G O Jones b Flintoff	26
S K Warne b Harmison	28
B Lee c G O Jones b Harmison	3
J N Gillespie lbw b Harmison	1
G D McGrath not out	10
Extras b5 lb4 w1 nb11	21
Total (40.2 overs)	190

Fall: 1-35, 2-55, 3-66, 4-66, 5-87, 6-126, 7-175, 8-178, 9-178.
Bowling: Harmison 11-2-0-43-5, **Hoggard** 8-0-40-1, **Flintoff** 11-2-50-2, **S Jones** 10-0-48-2.

M E Trescothick not out	4
A J Strauss not out	2
Extras lb4	4
Total 0 wkts (6 overs)	10

To Bat: M P Vaughan, I R Bell, K P Pietersen, A Flintoff, G O Jones, A F Giles, M J Hoggard, S J Harmison, S Jones.
Bowling: McGrath 3-1-5-0, **Lee** 3-2-1-0.

Day One – Evening session

Dismissing Australia for less than 200 before tea on the first day of the Ashes series left the England players jubilant at the interval, but their joy was to be short lived as McGrath chose the next hour to show just why he has been the world's best bowler for many years.

Lord's is a happy hunting ground for the lanky paceman and he showed why by claiming five wickets in a marathon 10-over stint that devastated England's innings.

In doing so he became only the fourth bowler in history to claim 500 Test victims – behind Courtney Walsh, Warne and Muttiah Muralitharan. The achievement came in a remarkable stint of five wickets for 2 runs in 31 balls to leave England reeling on 21 for five.

He reached the hallowed landmark with the first delivery after tea, slanting the ball across Trescothick for Langer to take the edge at third slip.

Four balls later McGrath's spell had begun to take hold with Strauss, his team-mate at Middlesex for a few weeks last summer, pushing forward and edging low to Warne at first slip.

With Lee providing both accuracy and hostility from the other end, there was no relief for either Vaughan or Bell as they attempted to rebuild the innings.

Their partnership was broken six overs later with a full-length delivery from McGrath keeping low to take the England captain's off stump. Bell followed in McGrath's next over, chopping on to his stumps off the front foot.

That brought together the exciting talents of Test debutant Pietersen and Flintoff – although at 19 for four it was probably not the situation they had envisaged. Their time together at the crease was brief with Flintoff playing all around another McGrath delivery that kept low. His wicket gave McGrath his third five-wicket haul in as many Test appearances at headquarters following his eight for 38 in 1997 and five for 54 four years ago. When McGrath was finally taken off some of the pressure went with him and Jones was able to dominate a determined sixth-wicket stand of 58 with Pietersen.

But with the close of a compelling day just two overs away, Jones' 84 minutes of defiance were ended by a brute of a short ball from Lee which he could only fend behind for Gilchrist to take the catch.

Giles followed for 11 in the final over to leave Pietersen on 28 after nearly two hours at the crease and a stunned England 92 for seven.

'To achieve this 500 milestone is something very special. I

The one they want. McGrath takes the prize scalp of England skipper Vaughan.

couldn't have asked for any more than to have the opportunity to achieve that at Lord's,' said McGrath afterwards.

'The first time I thought about it was at breakfast, which was surprising. I started to get a few butterflies in the stomach more in anticipation of the Test series. To finish day one with the 500 wickets under the belt was a great feeling.'

England's five-wicket pace hero Harmison could only marvel at the talents of the ageing McGrath, which overshadowed the Durham ace's earlier efforts.

'To get 500 Test wickets is a phenomenal achievement. I don't think Glenn McGrath has to prove any points. I'll be very happy if my Test career ends with 110 Tests and 500 wickets,' he said. 'He has proved that if you put the ball in the right areas, you will get wickets no matter what surfaces you play on and he did that.

'The team are pretty disappointed with the way the second half of the day went, but there is nothing we can do about it now. We've got to come out and get as many runs as we can and put Australia under more pressure with the ball.

'But, with the game as it is now, it is disappointing after bowling a team out for 190. Some might say we've missed a great chance – but they are a good side. If you bowl them out for 190 they are always going to come back at you.

'Sometimes you have got to give credit to the opposition and they came out and bowled well. Australia gave us credit for the way we bowled and we've got to do the same.'

ENGLAND: first innings
(Continued: 10-0)

M E Trescothick c Langer b McGrath		4
A J Strauss c Warne b McGrath		2
M P Vaughan b McGrath		3
I R Bell b McGrath		6
K P Pietersen not out		28
A Flintoff b McGrath		0
G O Jones c Gilchrist b Lee		30
A F Giles hit wicket b Lee		11
	Extras lb5 nb3	8
	Total 7 wkts (37 overs)	92

Fall: 1-10, 2-11, 3-18, 4-19, 5-21,6-79, 7-92.
To Bat: M J Hoggard, S J Harmison, S Jones.
Bowling: **McGrath** 13-5-21-5, **Lee** 14-5-34-2, **Gillespie** 8-1-30-0, **Warne** 2-1-2-0.

Day Two – Morning session

Pietersen seized the limelight at Lord's as only he can with another eye-catching display trying to keep England on competitive terms with Australia in the opening Test.

The one-day master-blaster hit a blistering 57 to guide England, who resumed the second morning trailing by 98 on 92 for seven, to within 35 runs of Australia's total and boost hopes of retaining an interest in the opening exchange of the Ashes series.

Not content with that contribution, which included hitting sixes off his Hampshire captain Warne and McGrath, Pietersen then displayed his agility in the field to run out opener Langer as Australia progressed to 47 for one at lunch on the second day.

Pietersen had resumed overnight on an unbeaten 28, an innings which demonstrated his great patience – not an attribute usually associated with the South African-born batsman – as much as the strokeplay which earned his call-up into England's Test line-up, and quickly set about trying to reduce Australia's lead.

Having blazed his way into international cricket in the one-day series in Zimbabwe and South Africa, Pietersen chose only his second morning in Test cricket to show he has the temperament to make the grade in the longer version of the game.

Before the series, much was made of his technique and how he would be able to adapt it to Test cricket. Undoubtedly, he is happier taking the attack to his opponents, but having shown on the opening day he can stick around he arrived at the crease on Friday with a totally different mentality.

He was fortunate to survive a strong appeal for leg before from Warne off the second ball of the day, which was rejected by umpire Rudi Koertzen, and showed his intentions by carving an early boundary off McGrath through the gap between slips and gully.

The need for that aggressive intent was underlined by the loss of Hoggard in the fifth over of the morning when he edged Warne straight to Hayden at slip for a duck, a dismissal which seemed to instil even more urgency into Pietersen.

In McGrath's next over Pietersen drove down the ground for four, before launching one straight into the Pavilion for six and then hammering through the covers for another boundary.

With the adrenalin now pumping, Pietersen pulled Warne over midwicket in the next over for six, but attempted to repeat the shot and was instead brilliantly caught by the diving Martyn just inside the boundary rope.

That was Warne's second wicket for 6 runs in only seven balls, but strangely Australia decided to replace him with the pace of Lee in an attempt to finish off the innings. Simon Jones and Steve Harmison had other ideas, hitting him for 13 in his solitary over from the Nursery End.

It was not until Lee switched ends to replace McGrath that the spirited 33-run last-wicket stand off 29 balls was ended when Harmison (11) chipped straight to mid-off to leave Jones unbeaten on 20 and England with a 35-run first-innings deficit.

Unlike the previous day, Australia seemed more cautious in their approach, although it did not prevent Hayden exploiting any loose deliveries and hitting Hoggard for 12 runs in his two opening overs while Flintoff conceded 16 in his first two overs.

It took another moment of brilliance from Pietersen to break Australia's opening stand, this time running in from cover to throw down the non-striker's stumps as Langer attempted a quick single in the sixth over.

But that did not affect Hayden's momentum, who progressed quickly to an unbeaten 32 at lunch – including five boundaries – as Australia moved into an 82-run lead by the interval.

ENGLAND: first innings
(Overnight: 92-7)

K P Pietersen c Martyn b Warne	57
M J Hoggard c Hayden b Warne	0
S J Harmison c Martyn b Lee	11
S Jones not out	20
Extras b1 lb5 nb5	11
Total (48.1 overs)	155

Fall: 1-10, 2-11, 3-18, 4-19, 5-21, 6-79, 7-92, 8-101, 9-122.
Bowling: McGrath 18-5-53-5, **Lee** 15-1-5-47-3, **Gillespie** 8-1-30-0, **Warne** 7-2-19-2.

AUSTRALIA: second innings

J L Langer run out	6
M L Hayden not out	32
R T Ponting not out	7
Extras nb2	2
Total 1 wkt (12 overs)	47

Fall: 1-18.
To Bat: D R Martyn, M J Clarke, S M Katich, A C Gilchrist, S K Warne, J N Gillespie, G D McGrath.
Bowling: Harmison 6-2-10-0, **Hoggard** 2-0-12-0, **Flintoff** 2-0-6-0, **S Jones** 2-0-9-0.

Day Two – Afternoon session

The second session of the day saw Australia make ominous progress towards a match-winning advantage, progressing to a comfortable 140 for three at the tea interval – a lead of 175.

Determined not to make the same mistakes as in the first innings, when their attacking approach resulted in them being dismissed for 190 despite winning the toss and deciding to bat first, Australia were more cautious this time around.

Hayden, having plundered boundaries during wayward opening

spells from Hoggard and Flintoff, played more patiently as the tourists resumed on 47 for one in the afternoon session. However, the former world record holder for the highest individual score in Tests finally allowed his attacking instincts to get the better of him. Unsurprisingly, it was Flintoff who made the second breakthrough just as the left-hander was looking to pick up the pace of his innings.

He had reached 34 off 54 balls, having hit five fours, when he attempted to pull Flintoff and only succeeded in bottom-edging the delivery on to his stumps.

That brought Martyn to the crease to join captain Ponting, but any hope England had of making another quick breakthrough were ruined by Simon Jones' inability to find any consistency.

Occasionally he produced a beauty of a ball to trouble the new batsman, but he was also guilty of straying too often on to the leg stump, which played into the hands of Ponting who set about laying the foundations of a sizeable target.

Ponting had scored a century on the same ground against England in the NatWest Challenge a fortnight before the Test series started and he again looked comfortable at the home of cricket.

He was content to accumulate steadily after the loss of Langer and Hayden, but one four off his legs from a Simon Jones delivery extended Australia's overall lead into three figures and moved him into the 30s at 85 for two.

After McGrath's 500th wicket on the first day Ponting then achieved a personal landmark of his own when he reached 41 via a single off Hoggard. In scampering that run he became only the seventh Australian to score 7,000 runs in Test cricket, reaching the feat in his 89th Test at an average of 56.

Harmison returned to the attack and Martyn carved him over the slip cordon down to the boundary to bring up the 100 in the 27th over and move himself into double figures, but Ponting's joy at scoring his 7,000th run was soon tempered – with a helping hand from an unlikely source.

Having manoeuvred his way to a careful 42 he slashed Hoggard straight to Somerset's James Hildreth at point, who was on as a temporary substitute fielder for Giles. Ponting had battled for over an hour and a half at the crease.

Clarke joined Martyn and the pair continued Australia's steady progress in taking the match further and further out of England's reach.

However, England could – and really should – have had another breakthrough just before the interval. Clarke, who had forged a determined 40-run partnership with Martyn, drove Jones straight to Pietersen at cover, but England's first innings batting star inexplicably could not hold on to the straightforward chance in the final over before tea.

AUSTRALIA: second innings
(Continued: 47-1)

M L Hayden b Flintoff	**34**
R T Ponting c Sub b Hoggard	**42**
D R Martyn not out	**24**
M J Clarke not out	**22**

Extras b6 lb2 nb4 **12**
Total 3 wkts (39 overs) **140**

Fall: 2-54, 3-100.
To Bat: S M Katich, A C Gilchrist, S K Warne, J N Gillespie, G D McGrath.
Bowling: Harmison 12-4-20-0, **Hoggard** 8-0-32-1, **Flintoff** 9-2-40-1, **S Jones** 8-0-30-0, **Giles** 2-0-10-0.

Day Two – Evening session

Pietersen was given a harsh lesson in Test cricket after Australia ruthlessly exploited his fluctuating fortunes to take command.

Applauded off the field after his entertaining 57 had restricted Australia's first innings lead to just 35 at the start of the second day, he was cast in the role of villain hours later when his costly drop of Clarke allowed the tourists to establish a potential match-winning advantage.

By the time stumps were drawn at the end of another absorbing day in the Ashes series, Australia had progressed to a 314-run lead on 279 for seven – already an imposing advantage even without the prospect of Warne and McGrath bowling in tandem on a wearing pitch in the final innings.

Reappearing after the 20-minute tea interval, the super-confident Pietersen had probably put his simple missed chance off Clarke behind him, but the story at the end of the evening session would have given him food for thought.

Clarke cashed in on the mistake and for the final two hours of the day England's general fielding deteriorated, with Hoggard allowing the ball to go through his legs for one boundary, Flintoff and Vaughan missing drives they should have stopped, while Pietersen's miserable afternoon was completed when his shy at the stumps off a no-ball flew to the boundary.

Clarke teamed up with Martyn to add a further 116 runs of their 155-run partnership spanning 34 overs, which took the game almost out of reach. Then England summoned enough determination and inspiration to claim four wickets for 24 runs in 51 balls.

Clarke had hit 15 boundaries to move within 9 runs of his third Test century when he chased a wide delivery from Hoggard and chopped on to his stumps via his back leg.

England quickly followed that unexpected breakthrough with Harmison winning a leg-before appeal against Martyn, who had battled for nearly four hours for his 65, with the next delivery and suddenly there was hope of an unexpected fightback.

Flintoff maintained England's revival by nipping a full-length delivery back on to danger-man Gilchrist's off stump and Harmison rocked Warne with a short delivery he could only fend off to Giles at gully with the final ball of the day.

Lifted by their final flurry, England left the field to another enthusiastic ovation, but their late rally merely papered over the cracks of a dire overall match situation.

Unfazed by that fact that England have only successfully chased 300 or more on three occasions in Test cricket, Pietersen was convinced England could change history.

'I think England have done pretty well in the last couple of years chasing in the fourth innings of a match,' he said. 'Tomorrow could be positive day for England if we get three early wickets. We can turn this around. They are only 314 ahead and we are in a good position to go on and win this game and change history. We must realise there is all that time left and that's a lot of cricket. As for the dropped catch, that is part of cricket. I'm not going to get too het up about it. I've got a job to do, we've got a job to do tomorrow. If I drop one tomorrow, so what?'

Unsurprisingly, Clarke had a different view on the match. 'We are in charge. We are 314 ahead and if we bowl similarly to the way we did in the first innings then it is going to be very tough for England to score those runs,' he said.

AUSTRALIA: second innings
(Continued: 140-3)

J L Langer run out	6
M L Hayden b Flintoff	34
R T Ponting c Sub b Hoggard	42
D R Martyn lbw b Harmison	65
M J Clarke b Hoggard	91
S M Katich not out	10
A C Gilchrist b Flintoff	10
S K Warne c Giles b Harmison	2

Extras b9 lb5 nb5 **19**
Total 7 wkts (70.2 overs) **279**

Fall: 1-18, 2-54, 3-100, 4-255, 5-255, 6-274, 7-279.
To Bat: J N Gillespie, G D McGrath.
Bowling: Harmison 18-2-4-35-2, **Hoggard** 12-0-46-2, **Flintoff** 19-4-84-2, **S Jones** 11-1-46-0, **Giles** 9-1-46-0, **Bell** 1-0-8-0.

'I think I owe Kevin Pietersen a beer or two for his dropped catch. I thank him for it, but that's the way it goes. Sometimes you catch them, sometimes you don't and fortunately for me I had a bit of luck.'

Day Three – Morning session

England began the third day knowing they needed quick wickets if they were to stand a chance of salvaging an unlikely victory, but they were held up by a stubborn Katich.

Already knowing they needed the highest successful fourth innings total to win a match at Lord's, England's task became more daunting after a frustrating third morning when Australia moved into an even more commanding position by adding 93 crucial runs.

Resuming already 314 runs ahead on 279 for seven, Katich hit an unbeaten 66 to guide his side to a powerful 372 for nine at lunch – an imposing 407-run lead which already meant England would have to score the second-highest fourth innings total in history to win.

England made the early breakthrough they needed thanks to a superb piece of fielding by Giles to dismiss Lee, who had been given a testing time by paceman Harmison and was struck on a hand by one lifting delivery which he did well to keep down.

He then received a similar type of ball which he played out to point, but was called through for a risky-looking single by Katich. Giles turned and in one movement sent a pinpoint throw to the non-striker's end which shattered the stumps with Lee well out of his ground after being slow setting off. His dismissal left Australia on 289 for eight. New batsman Gillespie leg-glanced Flintoff for four to ensure England faced the prospect of having to surpass their previous fourth innings run chase best of 332 – against Australia in Melbourne during the 1928/29 series.

Katich went on the offensive against Flintoff and struck him for three successive boundaries, two via the cut shot and a third which he leg-glanced to the Pavilion rails. Harmison was then guilty of straying down the leg side and Gillespie also helped the ball on its way down to fine leg as runs started to flow freely.

Flintoff was replaced by Hoggard after conceding 24 runs in four overs, but the new bowler was off-driven for 3 by Katich to extend the Australian lead past 350.

Harmison took the new ball, but immediately Katich pulled the first delivery for four, although when Simon Jones replaced Hoggard he should have ended Gillespie's resistance on 9 with his opening ball.

Gillespie edged the Glamorgan paceman through to Geraint Jones, but he spilled a straightforward chance away to his right.

Gillespie contributed 13 valuable runs, including three boundaries, to his partnership with Katich but finally fell two overs after his reprieve and 10 overs after England had taken the new ball. The tailender pushed forward to a seaming delivery from Simon Jones and lost his off stump.

However, even without Gillespie, Katich was able to expertly farm the strike to such an extent that he was able to add a further 31 runs before the interval with last man McGrath contributing a useful 10 to the 10th-wicket stand.

Katich completed his 50 off 81 balls with six fours.

AUSTRALIA: second innings
(Continued: 279-7)

S M Katich not out	66
B Lee run out	8
J N Gillespie b S P Jones	13
G D McGrath not out	10

Extras b9 lb8 nb8 **25**
Total 9 wkts (97 overs) **372**
Fall: 1-18 2-54 3-100 4-255 5-255 6-274 7-279 8-289 9-341
Bowling: Harmison 26-6-51-2, **Hoggard** 16-1-56-2, **Flintoff** 27-4-123-2, **S Jones** 16-1-61-1, **Giles** 11-1-56-0, **Bell** 1-0-8-0.

Day Three – Afternoon session

Faced with a record-breaking target of 420 to defeat Australia, England supporters were given some hope as opening pair Trescothick and Strauss gave the home side a solid start in the afternoon session after the tourists were eventually dismissed.

A staunch last-wicket partnership of 43 was finally ended when Katich sliced Harmison into the hands of Jones at third man after making a three-hour 67 off 113 balls with eight boundaries, leaving McGrath unbeaten on 20 and Australia 384 all out.

The last three Australian wickets had added 105 in 30.2 overs with the tailenders playing a key role, but they were aided by some slipshod fielding as England conspired to drop McGrath twice off the luckless Simon Jones.

Flintoff spilled an easy chance at second slip in the first over after lunch and then wicketkeeper Jones – with his second miss of the day – allowed another opportunity to go begging despite getting both hands to a ball McGrath had gloved.

Although Harmison's breakthrough 3.4 overs after lunch finally brought the punishment to an end, it left England facing a history-making chase.

Ultimate success for England would represent the highest ever successful fourth innings total to win a Test, eclipsing West Indies' 418 for seven against Australia in Antigua two years ago.

It would almost certainly rank as one of the greatest comebacks in Ashes history – especially on a wearing pitch against the combined dangers of McGrath and Warne.

However, if past performances were anything to go by, victory was the lowest of their priorities.

Athough Trescothick and Strauss did not look entirely comfortable, particularly against paceman Lee and spinner Warne, they negotiated 22 overs before tea to reach 65 without loss.

Trescothick's unbeaten 31 from 79 balls contained six fours while Strauss' 32 not out off 55 deliveries included five boundaries.

Warne only bowled two overs before the interval, but already looked as if he was going to pose the main threat after having confident lbw shouts against both batsmen rejected.

Trescothick was twice hit on the shoulder by successive quickfire deliveries from Lee, consistently bowling in excess of 90 miles per hour, while first-innings destroyer McGrath settled into his accustomed immaculate line and length.

Runs were initially at a premium and the first boundary of the innings did not come until the sixth over when left-hander Strauss cover-drove a rare loose ball from Lee.

England knew the importance of surviving the new ball after the

AUSTRALIA: second innings
(Continued: 372-9)

S M Katich c S P Jones b Harmison	67
A C Gilchrist b Flintoff	10
S K Warne c Giles b Harmison	2
B Lee run out	8
J N Gillespie b S P Jones	13
G D McGrath not out	20

Extras b10 lb8 nb8 **26**
Total (100.4 overs) **384**
Fall: 1-18, 2-54, 3-100, 4-255, 5-255, 6-274, 7-279, 8-289, 9-341.
Bowling: Harmison 27.4-6-54-3, **Hoggard** 16-1-56-2, **Flintoff** 27-4-123-2, **S Jones** 18-1-69-1, **Giles** 11-1-56-0, **Bell** 1-0-8-0.

M E Trescothick not out	31
A J Strauss not out	32

Extras nb2 **2**
Total 0 wkts (22 overs) **65**
To Bat: M P Vaughan, I R Bell, K P Pietersen, A Flintoff, G O Jones, A F Giles, M J Hoggard, S J Harmison, S P Jones.
Bowling: McGrath 8-0-19-0, **Lee** 8-2-29-0, **Gillespie** 4-0-12-0, **Warne** 2-0-5-0.

way they had capitulated in the first innings when they were reduced to 21 for five by the impressive McGrath.

Only 18 runs came from the first 11 overs but the scoring rate gradually increased after the introduction of Gillespie and the removal from the attack of McGrath, whose eight overs cost a miserly 19 runs. But then the boundaries started to flow at more regular intervals.

Day Three – Evening session

Warne emerged from weeks of turmoil and tribulations to once again undermine England's Ashes aspirations and put Australia on course for another emphatic victory.

Warne's build-up to the most eagerly-awaited Ashes series in decades was less than ideal, involving his highly publicised break-up with wife Simone, but he cast aside the upheaval in his personal life to deliver another telling performance and leave England praying for a miracle.

By the time bad light ended play with 10 overs lost, England were battling to avoid defeat having slumped to 156 for five needing a further 264 runs to claim an unlikely victory.

After McGrath had demonstrated his champion quality in the first innings, this time it was Warne and Lee in combination that accounted for England's top order.

England appeared to be progressing nicely as they resumed after tea on 65 without loss, but just 18 overs after the resumption Australia had taken five wickets as the pace and bounce of Lee and the genius of Warne sent them tumbling towards an inevitable defeat.

Strauss (37) was the first to go five overs after tea when he checked a pull and Lee reacted superbly to take a diving catch off his own bowling. Three overs later Trescothick (44) followed him when he propped forward to Warne and edged to Hayden at slip.

Bell was out-manoeuvred by the straight delivery which trapped him leg before in his crease to leave England captain Vaughan with the responsibility of halting England's collapse. Vaughan battled for 46 minutes for only four runs until Lee was recalled at the Pavilion End and struck second ball with a delivery which straightened and removed his off stump. Warne struck again three overs later to finish his good friend Flintoff's unhappy maiden Ashes Test with the bat when he was caught behind cutting off the back foot.

First-innings hero Pietersen chose to take on the Australian

Strauss
ducks away
from a short
one.

Vaughan's
second-
innings
dismissal.
Lee claims
the England
captain's
wicket for 4.

attack in his accustomed swashbuckling style and planted Lee well into the Tavern Stand before driving the dangerous Warne through the covers for four to reach an unbeaten 42 by the close.

On leaving the field, Lee insisted Australia were determined to inflict an Ashes whitewash on England and warned Warne was 'bowling the best he has ever bowled'.

'It is very hard to keep a true champion down. That's why he is a champion and he is definitely bowling the best he ever has. He is getting better with age,' he said.

'The batsmen appreciate they are playing the world's best leg-spinner and there is a lot of pressure out there as well. We have stated that we want to play some very hard cricket. We have come here to try to win 5–0.'

England vice-captain Trescothick admitted his side had a considerable mountain to climb if they were to salvage any tangible reward from the worsening first Test.

'We are disappointed. We got into a position where we were 80 for none and then we lost five wickets pretty quickly,' he said.

'We know it is not an ideal situation to be in but we will have to work hard over the next two days. We are obviously on the back foot big-time but you have still got to cling to the hope.

'You have got to work hard, stay focused on what we do. You can only hope that we can salvage something.

'You can only keep working otherwise we might as well give in now.'

ENGLAND: second innings
(Continued: 65-0)

M E Trescothick c Hayden b Warne	44
A J Strauss c & b Lee	37
M P Vaughan b Lee	4
I R Bell lbw b Warne	8
K P Pietersen not out	42
A Flintoff c Gilchrist b Warne	3
G O Jones not out	6

Extras b4 lb5 nb3 **12**
Total 5 wkts (48 overs) **156**

Fall: 1-80, 2-96, 3-104, 4-112, 5-119.
To Bat: A F Giles, M J Hoggard, S J Harmison, S P Jones.
Bowling: McGrath 12-1-25-0, **Lee** 15-3-58-2, **Gillespie** 6-0-18-0, **Warne** 15-2-46-3.

Day Four – Morning session

New England cap Pietersen's hopes of joining a select band in the record books were frustrated by the weather.

The Hampshire batsman began the day eight runs away from becoming only the eighth England player to score a half-century in both innings of his debut Test. However, that was about all the home side could look forward to as they stared at defeat upon being reduced to 156 for five the previous day chasing an impossible 420 for victory.

Pietersen top-scored with 57 in England's first innings of 190 and was unbeaten on 42 overnight, but persistent rain fell throughout the fourth morning to aid England's slim hopes of saving the game.

It ruled out any chance of play before lunch but it also halted Pietersen's hopes of continuing his impressive form.

Prince Kumar Shri Ranjitsinhji, George Gunn, Paul Gibb, Cyril Poole, Peter Richardson, Tony Greig and Strauss are the only other players to have chalked up two fifties on their first Test appearance. Strauss achieved the feat 12 months earlier when he scored 112 and 83 on his debut against New Zealand at Lord's.

Although the rain raised hopes of a draw, history was not on England's side.

Only 19 days of Test cricket had been totally washed out at Lord's in the past, the last being on the opening day of the England–Pakistan series in 2001, and in total 89 days have been completely blank in this country.

There was a huge burden on the shoulders of Pietersen and it should not be forgotten that although he made such an impact on the one-day tour to Africa, he had never been in this kind of position before.

The sustained pressure cranked up in a Test match is alien to Pietersen, but it was to him and wicketkeeper Geraint Jones, not vastly experienced himself, that England and the nation looked to as the last of the recognised batsmen.

The longer they could resist Australia, the longer delayed would be the entry of tailenders Giles, Hoggard, Harmison and Simon Jones. With these two batsmen rested the chances of denying Australia the chance to go one up in the best of five series.

Day Four – Afternoon session

With the entire morning washed out, hopes of play getting underway after lunch on the penultimate day of the opening Test improved when the rain finally ceased after five hours.

Umpires Aleem Dar and Rudi Koertzen made an initial inspection at 2.45 p.m. and planned another for half an hour later when the covers had been removed from the square. The heavens had opened shortly after 9.00 a.m., probably to the delight of the

England team who were facing defeat after slumping to 156 for five in pursuit of a 420 victory target.

It meant a long wait for first-innings batting hero Pietersen, who was 42 not out overnight, and Geraint Jones, 6 not out.

And despite anything the English batsmen, especially the super-confident Pietersen, may have publicly said about tackling the Aussies they were secretly grateful for the delay which made their job slightly easier.

But the reputation of Lord's for being one of the quickest drying grounds in the country meant there was every possibility of play later in the afternoon if rain did not return.

Day Four – Evening session

For once home advantage did not extend to the weather as the rain dried up, as did England's resolve with the bat, allowing McGrath and Warne to spark a quickfire collapse which hurried Australia to victory by 239 runs to go 1-0 up in the series.

England resumed on 156 for five after a four-and-a-quarter-hour rain delay and they folded without showing much resistance, to be dismissed for 180 with the last five wickets falling in the space of 46 balls.

Only Pietersen's second half-century of the match gave a few crumbs of comfort to an England side who had been outplayed since the first day, and the euphoria of dismissing Australia for 190 now seemed very distant.

McGrath, who had taken five wickets in the first innings, opened proceedings from the Pavilion End and he was immediately into a good rhythm with a maiden over to wicketkeeper Jones.

Warne, England's main tormentor on Saturday with three wickets, was also treated with caution by Jones and Pietersen, who resumed on 42 not out.

But then Jones threw his wicket away with an ill-advised pull shot to the third delivery of McGrath's second over. The Kent player succeeded only in lofting a comfortable catch to Gillespie at mid-on.

Jones had made only 6 and it completed an unhappy Test match in which he had also spilled two easy chances on Saturday.

England were then 158 for six – and two balls later it became 158 for seven as Giles became McGrath's second victim of the over. McGrath softened up the spinner with a bouncer and his next delivery prompted Giles to steer the ball into the hands of Hayden at gully.

The players returned to action after a 10-minute break for rain with Hoggard accompanying Pietersen out to the wicket for what was increasingly looking like a lost cause. Pietersen was being allowed to take a single almost anywhere to allow McGrath and Warne to try to expose a fragile-looking tail. But it was surprising he took that option in the early part of most overs rather than look to protect the lower order as much as possible.

The policy backfired when Hoggard completed an unwanted pair of ducks when he was adjudged lbw to McGrath from a ball which jagged back into him to leave England 164 for eight.

Pietersen had time enough to complete his second half-century of the match off 68 balls with five fours and a six, but then Warne got in on the act by claiming his first wicket of the day to have Harmison lbw for nought to the first ball he faced.

Pietersen showed some late defiance by lofting Warne for six over midwicket, but McGrath ended the match by having Simon Jones caught by Warne at first slip with Pietersen stranded on 64 not out as Australia won by 239 runs.

McGrath's wicket-to-wicket spell was four wickets for 3 runs off 23 balls, while Warne finished with four for 64.

England had not resumed until 3.45 p.m., but Australia took just 10.1 overs to complete another emphatic win at Lord's, where they are now unbeaten since 1934. It also raised fears the tourists would repeat their dominance of previous series.

That was something Vaughan was keen to dismiss. 'We've just lost to Australia, but we've lifted ourselves in the past and we've played some good cricket over the last two years,' he said.

'You don't just suddenly become a bad team, a team low in confidence, just because you've lost one game of cricket – we're only 1–0 down and there are another four to play.

'I think there's a real opportunity to go out there and play some good cricket against them. Australia will realise that during the first two days we put them under a lot of pressure and they certainly knew they were in a contest, but on Saturday and today we weren't good enough and we didn't handle the pressure as well as they did.

'Australia are a good side and they've proved that. The one thing you can't give a good side is a second chance. They've a good knack of taking the game away from you fast when you give them opportunities and that's what we did.

'It was the type of game where you really had to take the game by the scruff of the neck and at 100-odd for three we had an opportunity to take and we didn't take that and that was probably the story of their second innings.'

Australia captain Ponting, buoyed by the victory, believed Australia could complete a 5-0 whitewash.

'We've a good chance. We've a better chance now than four or five days ago. This Test match has had a lot of similarities to first Tests of other Ashes series and we've managed to go on and do that in other series,' he said.

'Have we broken the English spirit? I wouldn't think so. I think we have gone a little way to doing that, but I think they are a bit stronger side than that. I think they have proved that with some of their wins over the last couple of years. They are a quality side and I am sure they will bounce back and look to improve on this game in the next Test.

'But we don't have to improve. We just have to play the same brand of cricket from now on that we have in this match because it has been pretty good.'

Ponting also hailed the contribution of veteran bowlers McGrath, who finished with match figures of nine for 82, and Warne, six for 83 for the opening Test.

'They are two of the all-time greats of the game – with 1,100 wickets between them. What more can you say?' he said.

'Shane bowled as well as I've seen him – in total control. And Glenn's spell in the first innings was the turning point of the game.'

Australia win by 239 runs
ENGLAND: second innings

(Continued: 156-5)

K P Pietersen not out	**64**
G O Jones c Gillespie b McGrath	**6**
A F Giles c Hayden b McGrath	0
M J Hoggard lbw b McGrath	0
S J Harmison lbw b Warne	0
S P Jones c Warne b McGrath	0

Extras b6 lb5 nb3 **14**
Total (58.1 overs) **80**

Fall: 1-80, 2-96, 3-104, 4-112, 5-119, 6-158, 7-158, 8-164, 9-167.
Bowling: McGrath 17.1-2-29-4, **Lee** 5-3-58-2, **Gillespie** 6-0-18-0, **Warne** 20-2-64-4.

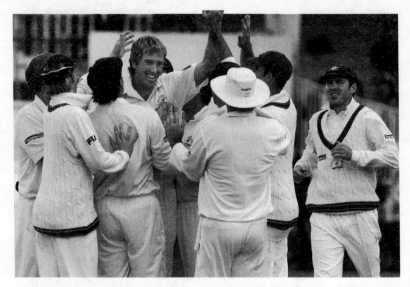

McGrath mobbed by his team-mates as he claims another victim.

Man of the match – Glenn McGrath

Many had questioned whether McGrath's status as the world's premier pace bowler, at the age of 35, was being maintained by former glories rather than present performance.

It was suggested he was becoming too long in the tooth and had lost another yard of pace.

Well, if he had, the England batsmen did not notice it. With Australia up against it after being dismissed for just 190, he produced one of the classic spells of seam bowling to spread panic in the home ranks.

During a marathon 10-over stint, he claimed five for 2 in 31 balls to leave England reeling on 21 for five. Fittingly, he also became only the fourth bowler in history to claim 500 Test wickets.

That spell set the tone for the remainder of match and achieved two things. It gave warning to England's batsmen that they should not be in any doubt about his ability to maintain his previous high standards.

It also sent a message to his own team-mates. For so long he has provided the lead from which they have followed, and an on-form McGrath eases the pressure on the likes of Gillespie and Lee while also giving Australia two world-class bowlers in him and Warne.

Man of the Match McGrath acknowledges the crowd's applause for yet another five-wicket haul at Lord's.

Although he did not add to his tally in the first innings, finishing with five for 53, he was far from a spent force.

In England's unlikely second innings pursuit of a 420-run victory target he was also the man who twisted the knife.

After losing two sessions of the penultimate day to rain there would have been an excuse for the lanky paceman not being on the mark straight away, but in only his second over he claimed two wickets.

With the tail opened up he moved in for the kill to finish off England in double-quick time, and his final spell brought him the incredible figures of four for 3 runs off 23 balls.

The era of Glenn McGrath was far from over.

McGrath at Lord's

Bowling: ....18-5-53-5 and 17.1-2-29-4
Batting: ....10* and 20*

Second Test Day One – Morning session

If England needed an omen before the start of the second Test at Edgbaston they could not have hoped for a better one than the shock withdrawal of McGrath.

The seamer was ruled out in bizarre circumstances after sustaining an injury in the team's pre-match warm-up on the morning of the Test in Birmingham and although no one in the England camp will have wished ill on McGrath, his absence undoubtedly handed the initiative to the home side.

Backed by the traditional hugely partisan crowd, England seized their chance to make amends for their woeful performance at Lord's.

Less than an hour before the start of play the Aussies were throwing around a rugby ball as part of a gentle pre-match session when McGrath trod on a cricket ball on the outfield and had to be helped from the field with an injured right ankle on a motorised buggy before heading to hospital for X-rays. Michael Kasprowicz replaced him in the starting XI.

The tourists were left to anxiously await the results of the scan, with the third Test at Old Trafford only a week away. Physiotherapist Errol Alcott said: 'Glenn has rolled his right ankle on a cricket ball during the early stages of this morning's warm-up.

'He was in considerable pain and had minimal movement so has been ruled out of the Test. We have sent him to hospital for X-rays and will know more about the injury as the day unfolds.'

The last time McGrath missed a Test match was in the 2003/4 season when he was recovering from an ankle operation and Australia won six out of their nine Tests during his absence, losing just one.

Since his return from that operation, though, the New South Wales seamer underlined his worth by taking 78 wickets in just 15 Tests at an average of 17.13, making him the leading bowler in the world since that comeback.

However, even with their No.1 pace bowler out, Ponting had no hesitation in asking England to bat after winning the toss. But without McGrath's new ball control, the home side made a comfortable start. Wayward spells from fast bowlers Lee and Gillespie enabled England to hit eight boundaries in the first eight overs and forge an unbroken half-century partnership in only 11 overs.

While Trescothick thrived, Strauss was fortunate to survive an early reprieve on 4 when he edged Gillespie low to Warne at first slip, who failed to take the catch at the second attempt as he fell backwards.

Trescothick was similarly fortunate on 32 after pushing at Kasprowicz in his second over and finding the safe hands of Hayden in the gully, only for umpire Rudi Koertzen to rule a no-ball for over-stepping.

That escape allowed Trescothick to reach his fifth Ashes half-century off only 74 balls, which included nine fours and a confident six when he punched leg-spinner Warne down the ground. Strauss became more positive on an Edgbaston wicket with few gremlins, despite groundsman Steve Rouse's pessimistic pre-Test forecasts after his preparations were ruined by a freak tornado the previous week.

The Middlesex batsman brought up his sixth century partnership with Trescothick with two driven boundaries through the covers off Kasprowicz, but fell in the over before lunch when a sharply turning Warne leg-break crashed into his stumps as he rocked on to the back foot to cut.

He was just two runs short of his half-century but played his part in an encouraging morning for England containing two sixes and 23 fours with Trescothick claiming 18 off the final over before lunch from Lee to finish unbeaten on 77 with England 132 for one.

ENGLAND: first innings

M E Trescothick not out..**77**
A J Strauss b Warne **48**
M P Vaughan not out **1**

Extra w1 nb5 **6**
Total 1 wkt (27 overs) **132**

Fall: 1-112
To Bat: I R Bell, K P Pietersen, A Flintoff, G O Jones, A F Giles, M J Hoggard, S J Harmison, S P Jones.
Bowling: Lee 7-1-43-0, **Gillespie** 6-1-24-0, **Kasprowicz** 7-3-25-0, **Warne** 7-1-40-1.

Day One – Afternoon session

If the morning session had seen positive cricket from England, nothing could have prepared the Edgbaston crowd for the fireworks that followed after lunch.

Flintoff launched a savage onslaught on Australia's under-strength attack as England fought back strongly from a mini-collapse.

McGrath's torn ankle ligaments gave offered England the opportunity to gain momentum and they enjoyed good fortune during the 112-run opening stand between Trescothick and Strauss, only for Warne's breakthrough to spark the loss of four wickets in 11 overs either side of lunch.

But Flintoff, teaming up with Pietersen for the first time in a meaningful partnership, shrugged off his personal disappointment from the first Test at Lord's to hit a blistering 68 off 60 balls and guide England to a promising 289 for four at tea.

The Lancashire all-rounder – who scored only 3 runs in two innings in the opening Test – hit six fours and five sixes during an unbroken 119-run stand with Pietersen spanning 21 overs, helping England to recover from a less promising 187 for four.

Flintoff was particularly severe with Warne, whom he dispatched for three of his maximum blows down the ground, and helped wrestle the momentum back away from Australia after England's top order again struggled to maintain the promising start provided by the opening partnership. Just six overs after the interval, Trescothick returned to the pavilion only 10 runs short of what would have been his maiden Ashes century – and his third successive Test hundred on the ground following his 105 and 107 against the West Indies in 2004 – when he nibbled at Kasprowicz outside off stump and edged behind to wicketkeeper Gilchrist.

Bell came to the wicket to a rousing reception from his home crowd and rocked back on to his heels to square cut Kasprowicz to the boundary.

But he lasted only three balls for 6 runs before playing forward to an outswinger – Gilchrist held on to the resultant catch. It was another Ashes disappointment for Bell, whose three innings in the series had brought only 20 runs. His departure also left England 170 for three.

England looked on course for another capitulation similar to that at Lord's when skipper Vaughan fell four overs later. Kasprowicz was taken out of the attack after a spell of 4-0-38-2 and replaced by Gillespie, who made a breakthrough with the sixth ball of his new spell thanks to irresponsible batting from Vaughan.

The England captain had moved impressively to 24 but after the loss of two quick wickets should have been looking to steady the innings.

Instead, the right-hander went for the hook shot against Gillespie and succeeded only in giving a steepling catch to Lee on the deep backward-square boundary.

His dismissal brought in Flintoff, who flourished in the football crowd atmosphere of Edgbaston, to accompany Pietersen and the pair were soon scoring at a rapid rate.

Pietersen pulled Gillespie for four to bring up the 200 in the 41st over and Flintoff struck Warne for two sixes over long-on.

Flintoff raced to his half-century in just 44 balls, smashing four sixes and three fours as Pietersen, unusually, was the man left in the shade.

But he provided great support for his more senior partner and by the interval was only 10 runs short of his third successive half-century, with England enjoying a commanding position.

ENGLAND: first innings
(Continued: 289-4)

M E Trescothick c Gilchrist b Kasprowicz	90
A J Strauss b Warne	48
M P Vaughan c Lee b Gillespie	24
I R Bell c Gilchrist b Kasprowicz	6
K P Pietersen not out	40
A Flintoff not out	68

Extras lb1 w1 nb11 13
Total 4 wkts (54 overs) 289

Fall: 1-112, 2-164, 3-170, 4-187.
To Bat: G O Jones, A F Giles, M J Hoggard, S J Harmison, S Jones.
Bowling: Lee 11-1-72-0, **Gillespie** 15-2-64-1, **Kasprowicz** 11-3-63-2, **Warne** 17-1-89-1.

Day One – Evening session

Pietersen reached his third successive Test half-century in as many innings for England but he was still out-shone by crowd favourite Flintoff as England amassed an incredible 407 on the first day.

Even though England were all out, nothing could dampen the party atmosphere inside Edgbaston as the home side showed they were not willing to capitulate, despite the crushing defeat in the opening Test.

England resumed after the tea interval on 289 for four with Pietersen – who scored two fifties on his Test debut at Lord's – and Flintoff having put on 103 from just 105 balls.

More was expected in the final session of the day and when Pietersen whipped Lee through mid-on for his seventh boundary to reach his half-century, there was a feeling that something special was building.

However, that anticipation was soon quashed as Gillespie

became only the fifth Australian to take 250 Test wickets when he had Flintoff – who had not added to his score – caught behind by Gilchrist.

England wicketkeeper Jones only contributed a single before he provided Gilchrist with his fourth catch of the innings, off Kasprowicz. That was the signal for Pietersen to go on the offensive, hitting Lee for three fours in an over, and he found a useful ally in Giles, batting on his home ground.

The pair added 49 in eight overs before Giles (23), who had survived two confident lbw shouts from Warne, was finally given out leg before to the spinner to leave England on 342 for seven in the 66th over.

Pietersen lofted Lee for a huge six over midwicket but in the same over finally perished for 71 attempting the same shot with Katich taking the catch. The latest star of English cricket smashed one six and 10 fours in his 76-ball innings.

Even after his departure, the hard-hitting skills of Harmison and Jones enabled England to add 59 for the final two wickets before Warne polished off the tail, claiming his fourth wicket of the innings.

Warne and Lee had both conceded over 100 runs during the onslaught, but with fewer than eight overs remaining, light rain prevented Australia starting their reply.

The total of 407 was England's ninth-highest first day Test score and their best effort since making 409 for five against Australia at Lord's in 1938. It was only the second time since the War they had surpassed 400.

In reaching such a daunting total they also ensured that Australia had to break Edgbaston history to win, as no side who had totalled 300 in the first innings of a Test at this ground had ever lost.

Andrew Flintoff said he had enjoyed a 'pleasing day'. 'I went out in a more positive frame of mind and it was nice to get 60-odd,' he said. 'After the Test last week when we struggled with the bat we are pleased with 400. If we are being hyper-critical we could have had more, but it was a pleasing day.' Pietersen added: 'I think it was a good day for us. It is never an easy game but when you are in the runs you have to try to take advantage of it.

'I am very happy with my own form and it is nice to reward people for the support I have been getting over the last few months.

'With 407 we have done a great job as a team. It is great to be part of the runs and see Freddie back in the runs.'

ENGLAND: first innings
(Continued: 289-4)

K P Pietersen c Katich b Lee..**71**
A Flintoff c Gilchrist b Gillespie **68**
G O Jones c Gilchrist b Kasprowicz **1**
A F Giles lbw b Warne **23**
M J Hoggard lbw b Warne **16**
S J Harmison b Warne **17**
S P Jones not out **19**

Extras lb9 w1 nb14 **24**
Total (79.2 overs) **407**

Fall: 1-112, 2-164, 3-170, 4-187.
Bowling: Lee 11-1-72-0, **Gillespie** 15-2-64-1, **Kasprowicz** 11-3-63-2, **Warne** 17-1-89-1.

Day Two – Morning session

Giles completed his week-long protest at his critics by claiming the crucial wicket of Ponting to provide a timely breakthrough for England in the morning session.

The Warwickshire left-arm spinner had spent most of the time since the 239-run opening Test defeat complaining about the level of criticism both he and the team received during their Lord's hammering.

But he bounced back strongly from what he described as 'a witch-hunt' by removing the dangerous-looking Australia captain just as England seemed to be running out of ideas of how to break a threatening second-wicket partnership.

Giles struck in his third over to end Ponting's brilliant innings of 61, which included 12 boundaries, after he got a leading edge to an attempted sweep and gave rival captain Vaughan a simple catch at short fine leg.

That breakthrough slowed Australia's impressive run-rate in the morning session and Vaughan's smart run-out of Martyn just before lunch restricted them to 118 for three on the second day.

A confident England, boosted by the previous day's boundary spree, had made an electric start with spearhead Harmison setting the early tone by hitting opener Langer on the helmet with the third ball of the day. The blow dazed the Australia opener enough to have him shaking his head for several minutes afterwards.

But it was Yorkshire seamer Hoggard who made the crucial early breakthrough, striking with the first ball of the next over by tempting Hayden into driving straight to Strauss at short extra cover. The Queenslander's duck was the first he had suffered in Test cricket since the Durban Test against South Africa in March 2002, a period spanning 68 innings, and gave England a flying start on an Edgbaston wicket still showing no signs of the uneven bounce that had been predicted prior to the match.

That early success was short-lived however, with Ponting teaming up with Langer in a brutal 88-run stand that threatened to take Australia into a commanding position by lunch.

Ponting raced to his half-century off only 51 balls but could have been dismissed before he had scored. He pushed Hoggard to cover, set off for a quick single and was beaten to the non-striker's end by Pietersen's throw, which flew narrowly wide of the stumps and on to the boundary for 4 overthrows.

After that early scare, Ponting dominated England's attack while Langer, who was also hit in the stomach by Harmison, played the back-up role. The pair raced to a half-century partnership in only 58 deliveries.

Jones briefly restricted Ponting's strokeplay as he began with two successive maidens after replacing Hoggard from the Pavilion End, but was taken for 13 in his next over with Ponting hitting three successive boundaries to reach his half-century.

But just as Ponting had his 23rd Test century and his fifth Ashes hundred in his sights, he played a lazy shot to Giles and set off back to the dressing-room while the England players mobbed their premier spinner.

Delighted at that bonus wicket, England were even more elated by a smart piece of fielding by Vaughan to run out new batsman Martyn with a direct hit at the non-striker's end from midwicket to finish off a successful morning. Langer, 27 not out, could only watch from the other end.

AUSTRALIA: first innings

J L Langer not out	27
M L Hayden c Strauss b Hoggard	0
R T Ponting c Vaughan b Giles	61
D R Martyn run out	20

Extras b4 nb6 **10**
Total 3 wkts (24.5 overs) **118**

Fall: 1-0, 2-88, 3-118.
To Bat: M J Clarke, S M Katich, A C Gilchrist, S K Warne, J N Gillespie, M S Kasprowicz.
Bowling: Harmison 7-1-35-0, **Hoggard** 4-0-26-1, **S Jones** 3-2-13-0, **Flintoff** 5.5-1-20-0, **Giles** 5-0-20-1.

Day Two – Afternoon session

Opener Langer dropped anchor for Australia to provide the backbone to their innings as he completed his second full session out in the middle to guide his side to 219 for five at tea.

Having watched from the other end as his team-mates employed some fluent strokeplay earlier in the day, the gritty left-hander made the choice to stick it out as long as he could as the tourists continued their pursuit of England's first innings 407. He returned to the crease after lunch at 27 not out patently aware he had to hang around and rebuild the innings after Australia lost momentum just before the break with two wickets in five overs. Langer is nothing if not a determined competitor with a very compact game and he reined in what attacking shots he has in his armoury for the sake of expediency.

He needed nearly three hours to reach his 50 – made off 93 balls with just four boundaries – but it was an invaluable effort on a slow pitch that demanded application.

Jones came back into the attack after the interval and Clarke, a player with a much greater array of strokes, was quickly into his stride with successive boundaries at the Welshman's expense.

Langer also came out of his shell to cover drive him to the ropes and the 50 stand between the pair came up off 74 balls. The fourth-wicket duo were gradually digging Australia out of a hole and into a position where they could again think about challenging England's big total.

The key for them both was to survive the session and hope to take advantage of a weary England attack in the final two hours, when runs are often scored at their fastest rate if two batsmen are well set.

But just as their stand began to threaten – and maybe their thoughts turned to reaching the tea interval unscathed – Giles answered his critics once again with a crucial breakthrough.

The Langer–Clarke combination had put on 76 from 117 balls when the latter pushed forward to a straight delivery and nicked it behind to wicketkeeper Jones.

Clarke had struck seven fours in his 68-ball knock of 40 and his dismissal left Australia on 194 for four – still 213 runs in arrears. Vaughan brought Flintoff back into the attack at the Pavilion End in an attempt to drive a decisive hole through the Australian middle order and, as is so often the case, the Lancastrian worked his magic.

Just five overs after Giles' breakthrough, all-rounder Flintoff, coming over the wicket to Katich, induced the batsman into edging behind three overs before tea and Jones claimed the catch.

Gilchrist joined Langer – who had moved on to 72 not out – for the tricky few overs before the interval, but even without further mishap Australia were still 188 runs short of England's first-innings total with only five wickets remaining.

AUSTRALIA: first innings
(Continued: 118-3)

J L Langer not out 72
M L Hayden c Strauss b Hoggard 0
R T Ponting c Vaughan b Giles 61
D R Martyn run out 20
M J Clarke c G O Jones b Giles 40
S M Katich c G O Jones b Flintoff 4
A C Gilchrist not out 5

Extras b4 lb5 w1 nb7 **17**
Total 5 wkts (53 overs) **219**

Fall: 1-0 2-88 3-118 4-194 5-208
To Bat: S K Warne, J N Gillespie, M S Kasprowicz.
Bowling: Harmison 11-1-48-0, **Hoggard** 8-0-41-1, **S Jones** 9 -2-42-0, **Flintoff** 10-1-30-1, **Giles** 15-1-49-2.

Day Two – Evening session

England claimed the upper hand over Australia after bowling out the tourists for 308, a lead of 99, and by the close of play they had extended their advantage by 25, although they lost opener Strauss in the process.

Spinner Giles and all-rounder Flintoff both claimed three wickets as Australia were dismissed in exactly 76 overs, but it was Jones who claimed the prized wicket of Langer, who had defied England for four-and-a-half hours in making 82 from 154 balls with seven fours.

Langer had shown guts and gritty determination as wickets fell steadily at the other end, but he finally perished when trapped lbw by a ball of full length from Jones.

The Glamorgan paceman produced a useful spell late in the day, reversing the ball to good effect, and it was that which finally broke Australia's resistance and ended Langer's innings.

The opener added 54 crucial runs with Gilchrist, and the partnership had begun to take on great significance, when Langer was given out to an inswinging yorker which may have missed leg stump.

That left Australia on 262 for six – still 145 in arrears – and much then rested on the shoulders of Gilchrist and new batsman Warne if Australia's likely deficit was to be kept within manageable proportions.

Australia needed Warne to bat responsibly and give Gilchrist the opportunity to guide them closer to England's total, but he did not look comfortable, playing and missing outside off stump to Jones on several occasions. However, he was bowled charging down the pitch at Giles to leave Australia 273 for seven and the world's best wicketkeeper-batsman left with the tailenders.

Lee followed 9 runs later, becoming the eighth man down when caught at slip by Flintoff off the pace of Jones, and although Gillespie provided 36 minutes of defiance, Flintoff wrapped up the innings quickly, gaining successive lbws decisions against Gillespie and Kasprowicz to leave Gilchrist stranded on an unbeaten 49 after two hours at the crease in his 100th Test innings.

With only seven overs remaining before the close, Australia needed a spark of inspiration to give them hope of mounting a fightback and Warne provided it with his second ball, a sharply turning leg-break which span almost the width of the wicket into Strauss' leg stump as he attempted to cover the timber with a stride across. It meant Warne became the first player to take 100 wickets in a single overseas country.

For Giles to finish with three for 78 was a good way to answer the critics who were unhappy with his performance in the first Test, although he said that was not his motivation.'I felt I had nothing to prove – certainly to myself. I think that is the wrong attitude to go out with. I always put myself under a little pressure and there is enough pressure anyway playing against Australia in front of a packed house,' he said.

'I'm not a big one for turning around and sticking two fingers up at people. I'm a bit better than that hopefully. I don't think I've stuck a finger up to anyone.'

Langer, however, hoped Warne's magical ball to dismiss Strauss – reminiscent of the famous one that accounted for Mike Gatting – would give England's batsmen a sleepless night.

'Hopefully that ball has put seeds of doubt into England's minds, not only for this game but for the whole series.

'If there can be a few Shane Warne demons that we can get into the England dressing-room, then all the better. He has bowled fantastically well to England over the years. If he can continue to do that, so much the better.'

AUSTRALIA: first innings
(Continued: 219-5)

J L Langer lbw b S P Jones..82
M L Hayden c Strauss b Hoggard 0
R T Ponting c Vaughan b Giles 61
D R Martyn run out 20
M J Clarke c G O Jones b Giles 40
S M Katich c G O Jones b Flintoff 4
A C Gilchrist not out 49
S K Warne b Giles..8
B Lee c Flintoff b S P Jones 6
J N Gillespie lbw b Flintoff..7
M S Kasprowicz bw b Flintoff 0

Extras b13 lb7 w1 nb10 **31**
Total (76 overs) **308**

Fall: 1-0, 2-88, 3-118, 4-194, 5-208, 6-262, 7-273, 8-282, 9-308.
Bowling: Harmison 11-1-48-0, **Hoggard** 8-0-41-1, **S Jones** 16-2-69-2, **Flintoff** 15-1-52-3, **Giles** 26-2-78-3.

ENGLAND: second innings

M E Trescothick not out...19
A J Strauss b Warne 6
M J Hoggard not out 0

Total 1 wkt (7 overs) **25**

Fall: 1-25
To Bat: M P Vaughan, I R Bell, K P Pietersen, A Flintoff, G O Jones, A F Giles, S J Harmison, S P Jones.
Bowling: Lee 3-0-13-0, **Gillespie** 2-0-7-0, **Kasprowicz** 1-0-5-0, **Warne** 1-1-0-1.

Day Three – Morning session

England's hopes of pressing home their advantage in the second Test disappeared in a flurry of wickets after Australia mounted a stunning fightback on the third morning.

Resuming with a commanding 124-run lead at 25 for one, but aware they must counter the threat posed by Warne on a turning wicket, England quickly slipped into trouble after fast bowler Lee claimed three for 4 in 11 balls to knock over the top order.

Their capitulation was briefly halted by a determined 41-run stand between Warwickshire batsman Bell, playing in front of his home crowd, and Pietersen. But Warne exerted his influence to take two for 1 in six balls and leave England reeling on 95 for six, just 194 ahead, at lunch.

England had begun the third morning cautiously with Trescothick and nightwatchman Matthew Hoggard – brought to the crease after Strauss's dismissal in the final over of the previous day's play – determined not to give Australia any early encouragement. But after adding just two runs to his overnight total, opener Trescothick fell to the 20th ball of the morning, bowled by Lee and

Flintoff was highly effective against Australia's left-handers throughout the series. Katich is on the receiving end here.

there began a capitulation as the fluctuating momentum of this Test again swung back in Australia's direction.

Trescothick was caught behind pushing at an outswinger outside off stump and giving a faint edge behind to Gilchrist, and three balls later Lee continued Vaughan's miserable run in international cricket.

The skipper failed to push forward to a fast, full-length ball which burst through his defences and removed his off stump for 1 – his eighth single-figure total in his last 12 international innings.

Lee claimed his third victim in his next over when he ended Hoggard's 34 minutes of defiance at the crease after the England man prodded forward and the ball found the safe hands of Hayden low in the gully via the edge of the bat.

At 31 for four, England were in danger of collapsing to one of their lowest recent Ashes totals, but once again Pietersen rescued the situation with some typically flamboyant strokeplay, including two sixes off Warne pulled through midwicket from outside off stump.

Bell, under threat for his place after just 20 runs in his first three Ashes innings, weathered the early storm and provided cautious support for Pietersen's more aggressive policy. Pietersen, perhaps lucky to survive an appeal for a catch behind down the leg side off the first delivery he faced from Lee, looked on course to claim his fourth half-century in as many Test innings after progressing impressively to 20 without further alarm.

But, as he attempted to force the pace against Warne, he was given out caught behind off the bottom edge and his pad as he attempted to sweep.

Warne then struck again in his next over when Bell pushed forward, edging the Victorian spinner behind to Gilchrist as England slumped to 75 for six.

Instead of continuing the collapse, however, Flintoff stood firm with a quickfire 17, although that may have come at some cost after he appeared to pull his left shoulder attempting to force Warne off the back foot. The injury brought physiotherapist Kirk Russell on to the field to administer treatment.

Jones was also given a reprieve before the break when Gillespie missed a looping return catch as England survived the remaining six overs before the lunch break.

ENGLAND: second innings
(Continued: 25-1)

M E Trescothick c Gilchrist b Lee **21**
M J Hoggard c Hayden b Lee **1**
M P Vaughan b Lee...**1**
I R Bell c Gilchrist b Warne **21**
K P Pietersen c Gilchrist b Warne **20**
A Flintoff not out **17**
G O Jones not out **4**

Extras nb4 **4**
Total 6 wkts (33 overs) **95**

Fall: 1-25, 2-27, 3-29, 4-31, 5-72, 6-75.
To Bat: A F Giles, S J Harmison, S P Jones.
Bowling: Lee 10-1-32-3, **Gillespie** 8-0-24-0, **Kasprowicz**
1-0-5-0, **Warne** 14-5-34-3.

Day Three – Afternoon session

Flintoff overcame a shoulder problem to produce some explosive hitting again as England set Australia a 282-run victory target with half the match still remaining.

The all-rounder had required treatment to his left shoulder during the morning session, but in the afternoon the Lancashire star took on the Australian attack almost single-handedly and smashed four sixes and six fours as he compiled 73 off 86 balls, before becoming Warne's sixth victim of the innings.

Simon Jones (12 not out) helped him add a vital 51 in 49 balls for the last wicket after the majority of the other batsmen had struggled to cope with Warne and Lee. Warne's return of six for 46 from 23.1 overs took him to within one of the 600-wicket milestone in Test cricket and it was the best analysis by an Australian bowler on the Birmingham ground.

It was the 30th time he had taken five or more wickets in an innings and he was admirably supported by Lee, who finished with four for 82 from 18 overs.

Lee had been brought back into the attack immediately after lunch as Australia looked to polish off the England innings, which stood on 95 for six at that stage – and he struck with the last ball of his first over.

Jones had guided Lee down through the vacant third man area to the boundary and then picked up a single on the off side to bring up the 100 in the 34th over. But he had made only 9 before he found himself back in the pavilion as he fended a delivery from Lee that went to Ponting at second slip.

Flintoff battled on and was pivotal to England's hopes of being able to set Australia a target in excess of 250 and he slashed Lee down to third man for a welcome boundary. Kasprowicz was brought into the attack for the first time in place of Lee after a five-over spell of 5-0-26-1 and Flintoff greeted him with a fierce pull shot to the midwicket boundary. But Warne struck twice in successive balls with Giles (8) caught at slip by Hayden and Harmison, for a duck, snapped up at silly point by Ponting.

With only one wicket remaining, Flintoff opened his shoulders once again and brought up his 50 off 63 balls with two sixes and five fours until Warne had the final say.

Flintoff hit both Kasprowicz and Lee for sixes to leave Australia having to make the highest score by a side batting in the fourth innings at Edgbaston to win a Test. The previous best was the 211 for three made by England against New Zealand in 1999.

ENGLAND: second innings
(Continued: 95-6)

A Flintoff b Warne	73
G O Jones c Ponting b Lee	9
A F Giles c Hayden b Warne	8
S J Harmison c Ponting b Warne	0
S P Jones not out	12
Extras lb1 nb9	10
Total (52.1 overs)	182

Fall: 1-25 2-27 3-29 4-31 5-72 6-75 7-101 8-131 9-131.
Bowling: Lee 18-1-82-4, **Gillespie** 8-0-24-0, **Kasprowicz** 3-0-29-0, **Warne** 23.1-7-46-6.

Day Three – Evening session

Having performed heroics with the bat, Flintoff did the same with the ball to help England close in on a memorable victory.

The big-hitting star – who went to hospital for an X-ray on his injured left shoulder at the close of play – followed up his explosive 73 from 86 balls before tea with three wickets as Australia chased 282 for victory.

Flintoff struck two massive blows in his first over to stun the tourists after openers Langer and Hayden had been relatively untroubled in reaching 48 without loss.

His second ball accounted for Langer (28) via the inside edge and skipper Ponting (nought) was caught behind by Jones from a ripping seamer.

It was the start of a dramatic slide for the tourists and by the close they had nose-dived to 175 for eight, still needing a further 107 to claim an unlikely victory – although Warne showed late defiance with two sixes off Giles.

Clarke falls to Harmison's slower ball.

England had their tails up and Hayden (31) edged Jones to Trescothick, who clung on to a fine one-handed catch at slip.

It became 107 for four when Martyn (28) clipped Hoggard to Bell at midwicket and then Giles put England in command with two quickfire strikes.

Trescothick held on to another slip catch to account for Katich (16) and wicketkeeper Gilchrist (1) lofted the Warwickshire player straight to Flintoff at mid-on moments later with a rash stroke.

The inspirational Flintoff then returned to the frontline to trap Gillespie lbw for 1. England were granted an extra eight overs to try to wrap up a three-day win, but Warne (20 not out) stood firm despite the dismissal of Clarke in the final over of the day.

Just when it seemed Clarke and Warne had stemmed the flow of departures with an eighth-wicket stand of 38, Harmison produced one of the deliveries of the series, a superb slower ball which Clarke (30) played all around as it crashed into his stumps.

Flintoff hailed it as 'the best day of my career' as England sensed victory. 'That is probably my best day in the game, especially at international level,' he said.

'If we finish things off, it would be the sweetest victory of my career. It is my second Ashes Test and hopefully my first Ashes win so it would be the highest point so far. It has been a great day for me.

'We believed that we could defend 282 and we stuck to our task. The atmosphere in the dressing-room is buoyant. After last week's defeat at Lord's we wanted to come here and put on a good show on and we played hard cricket and we are back in it.''

Even the veteran Warne was amazed by Flintoff's role in the proceedings. 'Freddie [Flintoff] was fantastic. He is a guy anyone would want in their side. He is a special sort of player,' he said. 'He has that "X" factor about him. He can lift a team around him and it is always nice to see Freddie do well. He is one of the good guys in cricket.' The leg-spinner added a note of caution for England though, saying: 'I'd like to think we are not finished. The beautiful thing about international cricket is that every time you walk through the gate you never know what is going to happen.

'There is something different every day – especially when you get the number one and the number two sides in the world playing each other.

'From Australia's point of view, it is very disappointing to be in the situation we are in at the moment because we fought so hard with the ball to get back into the game. We will fight all the way down. We will fight as hard as we can.'

AUSTRALIA: second innings

J L Langer b Flintoff	28
M L Hayden c Trescothick b S P Jones	31
R T Ponting c G O Jones b Flintoff	0
D R Martyn c Bell b Hoggard	28
M J Clarke b Harmison	30
S M Katich c Trescothick b Giles	16
A C Gilchrist c Flintoff b Giles	1
J N Gillespie lbw b Flintoff	0
S K Warne not out	20

Extras b8 lb6 w1 nb6 **21**
Total 8 wkts (43.4 overs) **175**

Fall: 1-47, 2-48, 3-82, 4-107, 5-134, 6-136, 7-137, 8-175.
To Bat: M S Kasprowicz.
Bowling: Harmison 10.4-3-26-1, **Hoggard** 5-0-26-1, **Giles** 11-1-52-2, **Flintoff** 12-2-34-3, **S Jones** 5-1-23-1.

Day Four – Morning session

England reignited their hopes of regaining the Ashes for the first time in 16 years when they completed a dramatic 2-run victory.

Stubborn resistance from the ten-wicket pair of Lee and last man Kasprowicz looked like taking the match out of England's reach.

But, at 279 for nine, Kasprowicz was caught down the leg side by Jones off Harmison to signal scenes of unprecedented joy from the England players and the capacity crowd.

Overall, England had bounced back in impressive style from their 239-run mauling at Lord's but, more importantly, would be taking the confidence from this performance into the third Test in four days' time.

It was only the second occasion that a side batting first had won in the last 14 Tests on the ground and Ponting was left to rue his decision to field first after winning the toss.

Despite the possibility of the game being over quickly on the fourth day, a sell-out crowd was present for the start of play and they gave Vaughan's side a huge cheer when they took to the field.

Australia were determined to make life as difficult as possible and Lee, who had proven himself to be an accomplished lower-order batsman, opened his account with the first ball from Harmison via a push into the covers for 2. But he was given a testing examination in the Durham man's second over and fenced three times outside the off stump at the towering paceman. Warne picked up the first boundary of the session when he rocked back onto his heels to square cut Harmison. But Lee was fortunate when he edged the same bowler over the slip cordon.

Lee looked more at home when he turned England's opening

seamer off his legs for four in an over costing 13 runs, and Warne brought up the 200 when he slashed Flintoff down to third man.

The ninth-wicket pair were looking full of confidence and Lee hammered Harmison for a straight four but, after adding 45 in 56 balls, Flintoff made a fortunate breakthrough when Warne, on 42, stepped back onto his own wicket to leave Australia on 220 for nine. Warne had struck two sixes and four fours in his 59-ball knock.

Harmison was replaced by Giles after a spell of no wickets for 27 from 3.2 overs, but last man Kasprowicz also looked full of determination. He straight-drove Giles for four and then steered the Warwickshire spinner to the third man boundary as the 250 came up in the 57th over.

The atmosphere became increasingly tense around the ground as Australia crept to within 20 runs of an unlikely victory after the returning Harmison had conceded four byes down the leg side.

Lee needed treatment on his left hand after being hit by Flintoff but recovered sufficiently to strike a four with an inside edge past his stumps.

England's last chance looked to have disappeared when Jones spilled a low chance after Kasprowicz, on 18, had sliced Flintoff down to third man with 15 needed.

But then came the incredible finale which left Lee unbeaten on 43 from 75 balls with five fours. Kasprowicz sank to his knees in despair after gloving Harmison to the wicketkeeper, having battled for an hour to add a crucial 59 runs with Lee, guiding Australia to within one streaky boundary of an incredible triumph at the start of the over.

While the rest of England's side hugged each other in celebration, Man of the Match Flintoff went straight over to Lee to console a fellow competitor after a thrilling duel.

This was Test cricket at its most compelling best and only one result – West Indies' one-run victory over Australia in Adelaide in 1992/93 – has been closer.

England win by two runs
AUSTRALIA: second innings
(Continued: 175-8)

S K Warne hit wicket b Flintoff		42
B Lee not out		43
M S Kasprowicz c G O Jones b Harmison		20

Extras b13 lb8 w1 nb18 **40**

Total (64.3 overs) **279**

Fall: 1-25 2-27 3-29 4-31 5-72 6-75 7-101 8-131 9-131.

Bowling: Lee 18-1-82-4, **Gillespie** 8-0-24-0, **Kasprowicz** 3-0-29-0, **Warne** 23.1-7-46-6.

Second Test reaction

Vaughan could only praise the character of his side after they held their nerve to prevent Australia completing one of the most stunning comebacks in the history of Ashes cricket.

Needing just 3 to win after somehow battling through from 175 for eight at the start of play, Australia's last man Kasprowicz could only get a glove on Harmison's short ball into his ribs and the grateful Jones claimed the match-winning catch.

'The nerves are there in that situation and there is not much advice on field placings for a captain when there are only 20 runs needed for them to win, but our lads showed character,' said Vaughan.

'They've played a good game under a lot of pressure against a good Australian side and it was great for Geraint to get the last catch – we've just got to produce two good performances back-to-back. That's the next challenge.'

Vaughan admitted England would not have recovered from going 2–0 down in the five-match series and he felt the influence of Flintoff was of major significance to the outcome of the match.

'I don't think we would have come back from 2-0 down against a team like this, the number one side in the rankings. It is fantastic to get back to 1–1. To get over the line is a real good boost. It sets the series up fantastically well,' he added.

'To beat Australia you need a real good team performance, which we had, but you also need individual brilliance and Freddie's performance throughout the whole Test has been outstanding.

'I've not seen a better all-round performance in a Test from Freddie than that. He has had some outstanding performances for us over the last couple of years, but to do it against Australia certainly is a fantastic achievement.

'He didn't score a 100 or get five wickets in an innings, but the two scores he made really gave us confidence and the last-wicket stand of 51 with Simon Jones in the second innings was the real momentum swing in the game.

'We could have been looking at around 230 to defend. To get it up to 280 swung the game back in our favour and Freddie gives us belief to go out there and bowl and get some wickets.

'There were so many twists and turns in the game, but both the last-wicket partnership and the first over that he bowled were turning points.'

Ponting insisted his side could be in an upbeat frame of mind for

Victory!

the third Test and that they should draw inspiration from almost pulling off a miraculous victory.

He said: 'That is the most nerve-wracking end to a Test I have played in. We had a great win against Pakistan a few years ago in Hobart when Gilchrist got us home when we were out of the game completely. This game is right up there with any game of cricket I've played in and that includes tied World Cup semi-finals.

'I feel pretty proud of the way we have played over the last couple of days. We've got very close to pulling off an unbelievable win and we haven't quite got there, but I actually feel quite happy at the moment. I was disappointed when you see the ball ballooning off the glove down the leg side and the game is taken away from you, but we can take a lot out of this game, especially what has happened over the last two days.

'Hopefully that can spur us on to playing some better cricket in the third Test when we will look for our top-order batsmen to score more runs.'

Man of the Match – Andrew Flintoff

Andrew Flintoff had been hailed as the world's best all-rounder and, despite decimating teams around the world with both bat and ball,

First Test, Lord's: The Aussies come storming back after a poor opening innings – in which they are dismissed for 190 – to leave England on 92 for seven at the close of the first day, with seam bowler Glenn McGrath taking five wickets – including that of Ian Bell for 6 (left)

There is no quarter given as the series gets underway, with Australia's captain Ricky Ponting (above) hit in the face by a delivery from England's Steve Harmison as the tourists are rattled early on

The Aussie bombardment continues on day two, with England's Kevin Pietersen having to take evasive action while facing Glenn McGrath

Brett Lee claims the wicket of England skipper Michael Vaughan (below) on day three as the home team slump to 156 for five in their second innings, needing a further 264 runs

England paceman Simon Jones shows his despair as wicketkeeper Geraint Jones drops Australia's Glenn McGrath during the tourists' second innings on day three of the opening Test at Lord's

Australia's great spin bowler Shane Warne torments England once again, including the dismissal of Ian Bell as the tourists head for a 239-run victory

Second Test, Edgbaston: Opener Marcus Trescothick (above) and all-rounder Andrew Flintoff (right) lead the England recovery, both hitting mighty sixes on the first day in Birmingham

England are back in business (facing page) as spin bowler Ashley Giles jumps for joy after defying his critics by claiming the scalp of Aussie skipper Ricky Pointing early on the second day of the second Test

England celebrate a dramatic victory (above) as Australia's last man Michael Kasprowicz is caught by wicketkeeper Geraint Jones off the bowling of Steve Harmison – with the tourists just three runs away from winning the match themselves

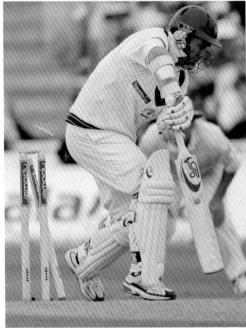

England's hopes of levelling the series at 1-1 dramatically improve when Australian opening batsman Justin Langer is clean-bowled by Andrew Flintoff

Third Test, Old Trafford: The Manchester crowd witness a piece of cricketing history as Australia's Shane Warne becomes the first bowler to reach 600 Test wickets with his dismissal of England's Marcus Trethcothick

The big screen at Old Trafford displays a congratulations message for the great leg-spin bowler after he reaches the special landmark

Third Test, Old Trafford: Michael Vaughan leads the way for England during his magnificent innings of 166 to guide his side into a strong position on the first day

England paceman Simon Jones celebrates taking the wicket of Adam Gilchrist as England have the Australians in trouble on day two at Old Trafford

there was the nagging fact he had not yet done it against the world champions – Australia.

However, in only his second Ashes encounter he showed he had the credentials to warrant the praise being lavished on him.

His arrival at the crease with England 187 for four could have seen the first innings go in one of two directions, especially batting alongside fellow big hitter Pietersen. The way he took the attack to Australia demonstrated to all he was not prepared to be dominated, even by Shane Warne, the greatest leg-spinner the game has ever seen.

One slight criticism would be that, having raced to 68 off only 60 deliveries, he should have gone on to make three figures, but anyone who witnessed him despatch Warne for six three times down the ground would defend him to the hilt. His 103-run partnership with Pietersen changed the tempo and the course of the game, and his help in polishing off the Australia tail strengthened England's position.

To repeat his feat with the bat second time around showed how his confidence had grown and the 51-run last-wicket stand with Jones was pivotal.

Just to enhance his image as the man with the golden touch, he then removed Ponting for a duck and halted Warne just as the tailender looked like he was going to win the match.

Flintoff's legend was growing.

Flintoff at Edgbaston

Batting: ....68 and 73
Bowling: ....15-1-52-3 and 22-3-79-4
Two catches

Close Test match finishes

England's 2-run victory over Australia was their narrowest winning margin ever. But only once has a team won a Test match by just 1 run, and again it was Australia who were on the losing end.

West Indies beat Australia by 1 run, Adelaide, January 1993
Tim May was Australia's unlucky spinner in the fourth Test, making 42 not out. But he ran out of partners in the home side's second innings when last man Craig McDermott was caught behind by Junior Murray off Courtney Walsh.

After drawing level in the series, the West Indies went on to win the decisive fifth Test by an innings and 25 runs as Man of the Series Curtly Ambrose ripped through Allan Border's side with a spell of seven wickets for just 1 run in the first innings at Perth.

Australia beat England by 3 runs, Old Trafford, July 1902
Australia clinched the Ashes in one of the lowest-scoring matches between the two sides. Having skittled the tourists for 86 in their second innings, with Bill Lockwood claiming 11 wickets in the match, England needed just 124 for victory

But they fell short as Australia won by 3 runs, with Hugh Trumble completing match figures of 10 for 128.

England beat Australia by 3 runs, Melbourne, December 1982
Allan Border thought he was playing a sensible game by turning down 29 possible singles during a 10th-wicket partnership with Jeff Thomson in Australia's second innings, and in many ways he was.

Protecting his partner whenever possible, the last-wicket pair put on 70 as Australia closed in on an improbable win, but Ian Botham then struck, having Thomson caught by Geoff Miller for 21 despite Chris Tavaré fumbling at second slip.

South Africa beat Australia by 5 runs, Sydney, January 1994
Shane Warne took 12 wickets in the match but Australia still lost. They had been on top until the final morning, when they resumed on 63 for four, requiring 54 more runs to prevail. Australia's collapse was shocking for the Sydney crowd, with Mark Waugh, Allan

Winning smiles: England hero Ian Botham (left) with captain Mike Brearley after victory at Headingley, 1981.

Border, Damien Martyn and Ian Healy contributing just 25 between them. Warne was run out for 1, and although McDermott flung his bat for 29 not out, Glenn McGrath was caught and bowled for just a single.

England beat Australia by 12 runs, Melbourne, December 1998
The Boxing Day Test at the Melbourne Cricket Ground, and after Alec Stewart and Steve Waugh traded first-innings centuries, the real drama came late in the match. Australia were set 175 to win, and were cruising at 130 for three. But Dean Headley took five consecutive wickets and Darren Gough finished the job with two wickets in three balls as Australia capitulated to 162 all out.

England beat Australia by 18 runs, Headingley, July 1981
England were famously quoted as 500/1 shots after slumping to 135 for seven following on, still 92 runs short of making Australia bat again. But then came Ian Botham's heroics which changed the face of the match.

He clattered 149 not out from 148 balls and Bob Willis then tore through Australia's batting line-up after they had been set 130 for victory, taking eight for 43. Probably the most famous Test match ever, and surely the greatest turnaround ever seen.

Third Test Day One – Morning session

Australia sprang a shock on the opening morning of the third Test at Old Trafford by including fast bowlers Glenn McGrath and Brett Lee – both thought to be doubtful with injuries – but it had little effect as Vaughan led the England batsmen with his highest score of the Ashes series.

Lee had spent two days in hospital in the week of the match in Manchester with an infected left knee, while McGrath was considered extremely doubtful after injuring right ankle ligaments treading on a cricket ball on the first morning of the Edgbaston Test.

However, the veteran seamer, who had still been on crutches earlier in the week, proved his fitness ahead of play, surprising even captain Ricky Ponting.

'It's astonishing to think he is back in the team after the way he looked a week ago,' he said. However, there was further injury concern for the Australians when Clarke was forced off the field in the second over with a sharp pain in his lower back.

McGrath almost had a dream return to action by nearly claiming the scalp of opener Trescothick in his third over after England won the toss and decided to bat.

Trescothick, still without a Test century against Australia in his 13th Ashes encounter, settled in with a turn through midwicket for 3 and a guide to the point boundary in McGrath's second over. He had progressed to 13 when he pushed forward to McGrath and edged behind, but wicketkeeper Gilchrist, diving to his left, put the chance down.

That reprieve enabled England to progress to 24 without loss after seven overs, but their unhindered progress was halted three overs later in the face of an impressive new ball burst from Lee.

Strauss had already survived one close shave, edging Lee just short of Langer at third slip after scoring 3, when he was given a reminder of the Australian fast bowler's express pace.

Lee, bowling from the Brian Statham End, dug a delivery timed at 88.9 mph in short and Strauss was beaten for pace as he attempted a pull shot and was hit below the left ear. It left the Middlesex left-hander stunned.

His 42-minute innings ended in Lee's next over when he lost his off stump to a slower ball that left England reeling on 26 for one with the out-of-form Vaughan striding to the crease.

This time, though, Vaughan was more positive and with

Trescothick playing equally well at the other end, they brought up the half-century partnership in only 68 balls.

Vaughan responded to his run drought by going on the offensive to hit six boundaries during his innings, including two in an over off Gillespie, as the hosts took advantage of good batting conditions. The England captain, who had scored only 32 runs in his previous four innings during the series, hit an unbeaten 41 in an unbroken 67-run partnership with Trescothick (35 not out) to guide his side to a comfortable 93 for one at lunch.

ENGLAND: first innings

M E Trescothick not out	35
A J Strauss b Lee	6
M P Vaughan not out	41

Extras b4 lb2 w1 nb4 **11**
Total 1 wkt (25 overs) **93**

Fall: 1-26
To Bat: I R Bell, K P Pietersen, A Flintoff, G O Jones, A F Giles, M J Hoggard, S J Harmison, S P Jones.
Bowling: McGrath 8-0-29-0, **Lee** 10-2-25-1, **Gillespie** 7 -2-33-0.

Day One – Afternoon session

The Old Trafford crowd witnessed a piece of history in the afternoon with Warne becoming the first bowler in history to reach 600 Test wickets, but the session still belonged to England, who progressed to 195 for two at tea.

Warne struck in his fifth over of the day to end a productive 137-run second-wicket partnership. He claimed yet another milestone in an illustrious career at the ground where he first established his place in Ashes folklore with the 'ball of the century' – his first delivery in England – against Mike Gatting in 1993.

Bowling from the Brian Statham End, Warne removed Trescothick after he mistimed an attempted sweep and the ball bounced off the back of his bat and rolled up the leg of wicketkeeper Gilchrist – needing three more victims at the start of play for 300 in his Test career – who grasped the chance. Warne was immediately awarded a standing ovation from the enthusiastic Old Trafford crowd and was congratulated by Vaughan.

Trescothick had continued to a determined 63 after taking 90 balls to reach his half-century and contributed towards a superb second-wicket stand with Vaughan after both players had survived early reprieves to exploit good batting conditions.

The Somerset left-hander and Vaughan were fortunate to escape after the luncheon interval. The captain had progressed to 41 just six overs after the break when he edged McGrath behind and, just as Warne was about to take the catch above his head at first slip, Gilchrist stretched for it and another chance went down.

His intervention ensured Vaughan collected another four runs after the ball flew to the boundary. Vaughan then lost his stump to a full-length McGrath delivery off the next ball, called no-ball by umpire Steve Bucknor for over-stepping, and England claimed another 2 runs from the deflection.

Despite those scares there were signs that Vaughan, who won the Man of the Series award in the 2002/03 Ashes, was finding his touch once again in mid-afternoon when he twice caressed McGrath square on the off side for four. He also took an aggressive approach to tackling leg-spinner Warne, using his feet and sweeping on his way to an unbeaten 68 in England's 151 for one at drinks. At this stage he had put on 125 with Trescothick (58 not out) as England attempted to further pressurise the Australians following the tense 2-run win at Edgbaston.

The productive second-wicket partnership added a further 22 runs before the batsmen were finally parted by Warne to leave England on 173 for two from 45 overs.

Vaughan – whose 50 had come up in only 64 balls – was 85 not out when he was joined by Bell and the Warwickshire batsman kept his captain company in the remaining 42 minutes before tea to put England into a commanding position.

ENGLAND: first innings
(Continued: 93-1)

M E Trescothick c Gilchrist b Warne	63
A J Strauss b Lee	6
M P Vaughan not out	93
I R Bell not out	14
Extras b4 lb3 w2 nb10	19
Total 2 wkts (54 overs)	195

Fall: 1-26 2-163
To Bat: K P Pietersen, A Flintoff, G O Jones, A F Giles, M J Hoggard, S J Harmison, S P Jones.
Bowling: McGrath 13-1-61-0, **Lee** 15-5-38-1, **Gillespie** 11-2-47-0, **Warne** 11-3-29-1, **Katich** 4-0-13-0.

Day One – Evening session

Vaughan exploited a succession of Australian lapses in the field to make his first significant contribution to the Ashes series with a superb 166 to guide England into a strong position.

Having struggled to assert himself with the bat in the series he finally broke the Aussie bowlers' stranglehold to reach three figures. He had entered the third Test desperately short of form after passing 50 only four times in his last 12 Tests with little sign of improvement, despite one-on-one sessions with coach Duncan Fletcher.

Resuming after tea, with Bell providing determined resistance at the other end, Vaughan began to resemble the batsman who brilliantly dominated Australia with three centuries two winters ago, and he became the first player of the series to reach three figures.

Perhaps it was the return to the ground where he made the first of his Test centuries – against Pakistan four years ago – that helped him settle down, but he looked a more composed and controlled figure at the crease than he had done scoring 32 in his previous four innings in the series.

Australia's fielding took a further turn for the worst with Bell being missed on 18 when he spooned up a return catch to McGrath after he had outwitted him with a slower ball.

Vaughan was also given another life on 141 when he pushed forward to Warne and was missed at slip by Hayden, which enabled him to pass 150 and keep the first double-century of his career in his sights.

Just 14 overs before the close, however, Vaughan's impeccable shot selection deserted him briefly when he strode down the wicket and launched Katich straight to McGrath at long-on having hit a six and 21 fours in his brilliant innings.

Pietersen played an equally ill-timed shot to the second delivery with the new ball from Lee and was caught on the midwicket boundary and the use of Hoggard as nightwatchman lasted 10 balls before the plan backfired, with Lee removing his off stump in the final over of the day as England closed on 341 for five.

The 30-year-old Vaughan classed his century – his fourth in eight Test appearances against Australia – as his best Ashes innings.

'I would say this is my best against them because it is 1–1 in the series and it really counts,' Vaughan said. 'I felt my luck was going to change and the run of low scores would end. You can also make your own luck and I think I have warranted a little bit – I didn't bowl the no-ball or drop the catches. I can only control my own batting, I played on instinct and I am glad it paid off.'

Although Vaughan's century stole the limelight from Warne's 600th Test wicket somewhat, the Australian was delighted to have cemented his place in history. 'I am pretty proud of that achievement, it is always nice to be the first to a landmark,' said the

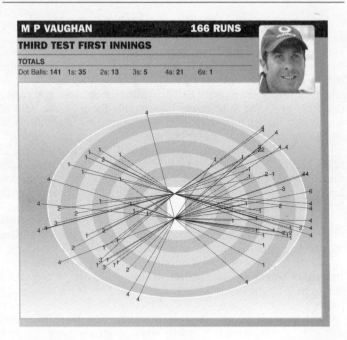

M P VAUGHAN   **166 RUNS**

THIRD TEST FIRST INNINGS

TOTALS

Dot Balls: **141**   1s: **35**   2s: **13**   3s: **5**   4s: **21**   6s: **1**

leg-spinner. 'I have been very lucky to achieve so many things on the cricket field. It has been an amazing ride.

'When I got 300 wickets, [bowling coach] Terry Jenner said I could get 600 and I asked him if he had been drinking all day. He probably had been!

'To do it at this ground is obviously pretty special as well with my parents here to top it off.'

Vaughan, who would have become victim number 601 but for a drop at slip by Hayden, added: 'He is a true great, but he can stop at 600 now. He's got enough! He is always a real competitor to play against and it is good to test yourself against the best.'

ENGLAND: first innings
(Continued: 341-5)

M P Vaughan c McGrath b Katich	**166**
I R Bell not out	**59**
K P Pietersen c Sub b Lee	**21**
M J Hoggard b Lee	**4**
Extras b4 lb3 w2 nb13	**22**
Total 5 wkts (89 overs)	**341**

Fall: 1-26, 2-163, 3-290, 4-333, 5-341.
To Bat: A Flintoff, G O Jones, A F Giles, S J Harmison, S P Jones.
Bowling: McGrath 19-3-76-0, **Lee** 19-6-58-3, **Gillespie** 15-2-89-0, **Warne** 27-5-75-1, **Katich** 9-1-36-1.

Vaughan salutes the crowd.

Day Two – Morning session

An enterprising seventh-wicket stand of 87 between local hero Flintoff and Jones prevented an England collapse on the second morning as nemesis Warne claimed his 150th wicket in Ashes battles.

Resuming on 341 for five the hosts lost Bell early on, dismissed for his overnight score of 59 after being adjudged caught behind hooking at a bouncer.

Umpire Steve Bucknor took an eternity to raise his finger and television replays of the dismissal did not provide conclusive evidence that the ball had brushed the gloves.

Only the healthy seventh-wicket stand between Flintoff and Jones pushed England beyond 400, but when both fell shortly before lunch, England were 434 for eight.

Flintoff had got going with an edge for four off Lee in the second over of the day and then forced another four off the back foot off McGrath as England progressed to 376 for six. Jones began with an edge to the rope at third man.

Warne was introduced after 50 minutes of play but his first over was sent down in heavy rain and play was stopped moments later in the middle of a Lee over.

Play was only held up for 20 minutes, however, and England attacked upon the resumption as Flintoff and Jones shared a half-century stand. Wicketkeeper Jones used his feet to hit Warne over the top for four while both batsmen struck boundaries off Lee in an over that cost 13. That saw the end of Lee, Australia's main threat, after eight overs in the session at a cost of 48. England's positive approach cost them though as Flintoff fell 4 runs short of a third successive half-century when he miscued an audacious blow off Warne to be held at long-on by Langer – his 150th English Test victim. Flintoff's quickfire 46 came off 67 balls, including seven fours.

Moments later Jones (42) followed when the out-of-sorts Gillespie crept one through a defensive push to topple off stump.

ENGLAND: first innings
(Continued: 341-5)

I R Bell c Gilchrist b Lee	59
A Flintoff c Langer b Warne	46
G O Jones b Gillespie	42
A F Giles not out	0
Extras b4 lb5 w3 nb15	27
Total 8 wkts (110.2 overs)	434

Fall: 1-26 2-163 3-290 4-333 5-341 6-346 7-433 8-434.
To Bat: S J Harmison, S P Jones.
Bowling: McGrath 25-6-86-0, Lee 27-6-100-4, **Gillespie** 17.2-2-105-1, **Warne** 32-5-98-2, Katich 9-1-36-1.

Day Two – Afternoon session

England's collapse continued after the interval with their final two wickets falling in the first three overs. Warne claimed both to finish with four for 99, but the home side still had the advantage by the end of the session with Australia 73 for one – 371 behind.

For once there was no resistance from England's tail with Giles being caught by Hayden and Jones bowled by the leg-spinner as just 10 runs were added to the lunch score of 434 for eight.

Australia started their reply knowing they had to reshuffle their batting order because of Clarke's back trouble, which had kept him off the field from the second over on Thursday and ensured he could not bat before number seven because of the amount of time he had been absent.

Both Langer and Hayden started positively, but Hoggard failed to grasp an early chance to undermine their response. The Yorkshire swing bowler got his right hand to a return catch offered by Hayden in the sixth over of the innings, but could not hold on.

There were few other signs of a breakthrough, however, other than a confident leg-before shout from Hoggard in his first over when the ball swung back into the left-hander but was adjudged to be missing leg stump.

Hayden's opening partner, Langer, cover-drove confidently and the 50 came up in the 13th over despite the helpful overhead conditions – beating Australia's previous best opening stand of the series of 46.

ENGLAND: first innings
(Continued: 434-8)

A F Giles c Hayden b Warne 0
S J Harmison not out... 10
S P Jones b Warne 0

Extras b4 lb5 w3 nb15 **27**
Total (113.2 overs) **444**

Fall: 1-26, 2-163, 3-290, 4-333, 5-341, 6-346, 7-433, 8-434, 9-438.
Bowling: McGrath 25-6-86-0, **Lee** 27-6-100-4, **Gillespie** 19-2-114-1, **Warne** 33.2-5-99-4, **Katich** 9-1-36-1.

AUSTRALIA: first innings

J L Langer c Bell b Giles 31
M L Hayden not out... 33
R T Ponting not out 7

Extras lb1 nb1 **2**
Total 1 wkt (20 overs) **73**

Fall: 1-58
To Bat: D R Martyn, M J Clarke, S M Katich, A C Gilchrist, S K Warne, J N Gillespie, G D McGrath.
Bowling: Harmison 3-0-15-0, **Hoggard** 6-2-22-0, **Flintoff** 5-0-20-0, **S P Jones** 3-1-3-0, **Giles** 3-1-12-1.

It was not until England's third bowling change, which brought Giles into the attack, that they were able to stem the flow of runs. Warwickshire's left-arm spinner struck a timely blow with his fifth ball from the Brian Statham End and Langer, pushing towards the leg side, was brilliantly caught at short leg by Bell with the total on 58.

Captain Ponting joined Hayden and the pair kept England at bay until the tea interval.

Day Two – Evening session

Unsung duo Giles and Jones bowled England into a strong position with three wickets apiece as Australia struggled to 210 for seven by the close on the second day, still 234 runs behind.

Each enjoyed regular successes after the Australians had looked well placed after resuming their response in the final session at 73 for one. Only Warne offered lengthy resistance for the tourists as the majority of the top six got starts but failed to kick on.

Jones claimed the prize scalp of Ponting with the first ball after tea. The delivery rose sharply from short of a length and looped to Bell at gully.

Three overs later Giles' increasing influence on the fluctuating fortunes of the day became apparent when Hayden, who had battled for nearly two hours for his 34, was given leg before to a turning delivery on the back foot. It left Australia 82 for three and already in trouble.

A back injury to Clarke pushed Katich one place up the order and he combined with Martyn in a key 33-run stand which appeared to have stabilised Australia's innings. However, Katich shouldered arms to the first delivery after a drinks break and lost his off stump to Flintoff.

Martyn followed three overs later, beaten by Giles' turn as he pushed forward defensively with the ball clipping the top of off stump. Giles continued his spell for the remainder of the day from that end while Vaughan shuffled his impressive pack of seamers with Flintoff and Jones being given the responsibility to make further inroads.

Gilchrist once again played a restrained innings, taking 74 minutes to score 30 runs, and had looked capable of making England pay for dropping him twice off one over from Flintoff for 12 and 13. Yet to score a half-century in the series, perhaps because of the pressure imposed by Australia's struggling top order, Gilchrist was first reprieved by Bell, failing to take a sharp catch in the gully, and two balls later he drove hard to cover where Pietersen fluffed the chance.

But once again the first ball of a new spell unsettled Gilchrist and he edged Jones behind just six overs before the close. He was followed four overs later by Clarke, batting with a runner, who lofted the same bowler straight to Flintoff at mid-off.

Only a hard-hitting 45 from Warne spared the Australians' blushes as they closed the second day under real pressure, but despite gaining the upper hand, Giles said England had to press home their advantage.

'We cannot ease off the accelerator, this is crunch time and this Test match is vital,' said Giles, who finished with three for 66 from 21 overs on the reel from the Warwick Road End.

'We are only two and a half Tests through the series and we have to keep coming out hard as they are a side that like to dominate. That means we have to continue to play aggressive cricket.'

Australia coach John Buchanan clung to the hope of a fightback akin to the one that got the tourists to within a scoring shot of victory in Birmingham, but admitted Vaughan's team were executing their plans with precision.

'We are behind at this stage of the game but as we saw at Edgbaston there is always quite a bit of fight in the Australian cricket team,' he said.

'We have got three days to turn it around. At the moment, England are taking wickets at key times so that the next player in is not as free to play as he would like. That impacts on a way a team plays but credit to England for what they have done.'

AUSTRALIA: first innings
(Continued: 73-1)

M L Hayden lbw b Giles	**34**
R T Ponting c Bell b S P Jones	**7**
D R Martyn b Giles	**20**
S M Katich b Flintoff	**17**
A C Gilchrist c G O Jones b S P Jones	**30**
S K Warne not out	**45**
M J Clarke c Flintoff b S P Jones	**7**
J N Gillespie not out	**4**

Extras b4 lb5 w2 nb8 **15**
Total 7 wkts (56 overs) **210**

Fall: 1-58 2-73 3-82 4-115 5-129 6-182 7-197.
To Bat: G D McGrath.
Bowling: Harmison 6-0-37-0, **Hoggard** 6-2-22-0, **Flintoff** 12-0-46-1, **S P Jones** 11-3-34-3, **Giles** 21-3-66-3.

Day Three – Morning and Afternoon sessions

Rain stalled England's Ashes momentum by delaying the start of the third day's play. The hosts had been hoping to consolidate a highly promising position after reducing Australia to 210 for seven in reply to their own first innings 444.

With rain still falling in the morning but predicted to clear from the north-west, prospects of play were poor before lunch but significantly improved afterwards.

Prospects of some play increased at 10.30 a.m. with the ground-staff taking the covers off the wicket and beginning preparations to mop up the playing area and with play possible until 7 p.m. they were hopeful of having some action during the day.

But the rain soon returned and, with it persisting, umpires Billy Bowden and Steve Bucknor opted to take an early lunch at midday.

The weather, so often a saviour for England in the past, was definitely helping their opponents this time as the entire afternoon session fell foul of the rain.

Bucknor and Bowden made another inspection at 3:30 p.m. and decided play could begin at 4 p.m. – with 38 overs left in the day – in the event of no further rain. Despite being unable to take the field so far on day three, Australia's match situation changed marginally for the better when it was decided they had been short-changed by 4 runs the previous day.

Bucknor failed to signal 4 byes which came off a Jones no-ball to Hayden. After the runs had been belatedly added, Australia's total went up to 214 for seven – meaning they needed only another 31 to pass the follow-on mark.

Day Three – Evening session

England fluffed the chance to strengthen their advantage on the third Test following another inconsistent wicketkeeping display from Jones in between the showers.

Restricted to only 14 overs during a rain-affected day, England would have hoped to have made further inroads into Australia's line-up after they resumed 230 runs adrift on 214 for seven.

But instead of grasping their opportunities – as they had done so successfully during the opening two days – this time they were unable to take them with Jones the big culprit as Australia reached 264 for seven by the close.

Needing 31 runs to avoid the prospect of following on for the first time in 17 years and the first time in an Ashes Test since 1986, Australia's hopes hinged on Warne progressing to his half-century and beyond.

But twice, including once before Australia had saved the follow-on, Jones allowed him to escape and he finished unbeaten on 78 in sight of his first century in his 126th Test after adding a crucial 50 runs with Gillespie in the play available. Warne had already had one reprieve after reaching 51, when he came down the wicket to Giles and drove hard down the pitch. The ball narrowly evaded the England spinner's outstretched hand, clipped the top of the stumps and flew to the boundary.

Australia were still 13 runs adrift of reaching their follow-on target of 245 at that stage and Warne was gifted another chance off the very next ball when he again advanced down the pitch. This time Giles beat him with the turn, only for Jones to fluff a regulation stumping.

The importance of that miss was underlined with Warne driving down the ground for four in Giles' next over to save the follow-on before the rain once again intervened and caused a halt after eight overs and 32 minutes' play.

Jones had clearly not recovered his composure during the 100-minute delay before play began again because, three overs after the re-start, Warne pushed forward to Flintoff and edged behind to give a routine catch at waist height. Jones did not need to move to take it and got both gloves behind the ball but he embarrassingly fumbled and allowed Warne to escape for a second time.

That blunder took Jones' tally of mistakes in 18 Tests to a disappointing 10 dropped catches and three missed stumpings while he has conceded 189 byes during the same period.

Asked how crucial the missed opportunities were, coach Duncan Fletcher said: 'It's important. You don't want to miss any chances at this level and we've missed some today. Anyone who drops catches is going to be upset and he's [Jones] got to make sure that he has the character to handle that.

'They are chances that Geraint would expect to take but, every now and again, you are going to have a few lapses. I have watched a lot of cricket when I am not with England and I have seen Gilchrist drop them, Mark Boucher [South Africa's wicketkeeper] drop many, Kumar Sangakkara drop many for Sri Lanka and 'keepers for India do the same.

'Most of the sides around the world want to go for a batter that can keep wicket and if you go for that policy you have to expect a couple of chances to go begging.'

Australia, meanwhile, were confident Clarke would be closer to full fitness after a back spasm should he be required to bat again. 'He is coming along nicely,' said physio Errol Alcott.

'He is now moving a bit more freely. There are signs that he is not 100 per cent yet, but we are aiming for him to be unencumbered with his back pain so he can play his shots.'

AUSTRALIA: first innings
(Continued: 214-7)

S K Warne not out 78
J N Gillespie not out 7

Extras b8 lb7 w8 nb10 **33**
Total 7 wkts (70 overs) **264**
Fall: 1-58, 2-73, 3-86, 4-119, 5-133, 6-186, 7-201.
To Bat: G D McGrath.
Bowling: Harmison 6-0-37-0, **Hoggard** 6-2-22-0, **Flintoff** 17-1-54-1, **S P Jones** 13-3-43-3, **Giles** 28-4-93-3.

Day Four – Morning session

England overcame the loss of nearly all of Saturday to rain to end Australia's resistance and claim a healthy 142-run first-innings lead.

Resuming 180 runs adrift on 264 for seven, the tourists had hoped to frustrate England for as long as possible with Warne aiming for a maiden Test century.

But Warne and Australia were blown away by a stunning burst of three for 6 in 29 balls by seamer Jones, who claimed Test-best figures of six for 53.

Jones' return was the best by an England bowler in an Old Trafford Ashes Test since Jim Laker's record-breaking haul of 10 for 53 in the 1956 Test, and helped dismiss Australia for 302 to earn a healthy lead, which was increased to 168 runs by lunch when England reached 26 without loss.

Jones' first ball of the day was clouted through the off side by Warne for four but the next, pitched halfway down the track, was hooked to deep square leg – straight to Giles which meant Warne fell 10 runs short of his ton after hitting 11 fours and a six.

Lee, whose determined 43 almost saved the last Test, fell four overs later after being given a working over with a nasty bouncer. Jones followed this up with one on a probing line outside off stump. Lee edged behind and Trescothick took a superb diving catch at slip.

A rare display of aggression from Gillespie, when he hooked Jones into the stands at long leg to bring up the 300, encouraged Vaughan to take the new ball.

Jones finished the Australian innings with the third delivery with the new ball, winning a leg-before decision against Gillespie.

Facing a tricky eight overs before the interval, opener Strauss twice had narrow escapes. First he edged McGrath behind but the chance fell just short of Ponting at second slip.

Three overs later he was fortunate again when he edged Lee between Warne and Ponting at first and second slip to collect his first boundary but finished unbeaten on 10 at lunch while Trescothick reached 12.

AUSTRALIA: first innings
(Continued: 264-7)

S K Warne c Giles b S Jones	90
J N Gillespie lbw b SJones	26
B Lee c Trescothick b S Jones	1
G D McGrath not out	1

Extras b8 lb7 w8 nb15 **38**
Total (84.5 overs) **302**
Fall: 1-58, 2-73, 3-86, 4-119, 5-133, 6-186, 7-201, 8-287, 9-293.
Bowling: Harmison 10-0-47-0, Hoggard 6-2-22-0, **Flintoff** 20-1-65-1, **S Jones** 17.5-6-53-6, **Giles** 31-4-100-3.

ENGLAND: second innings

M E Trescothick not out	12
A J Strauss not out	10

Extras lb1 nb3 **4**
Total 0 wkts (8 overs) **26**
To Bat: M P Vaughan, I R Bell, K P Pietersen, A Flintoff, G O Jones, A F Giles, M J Hoggard, S J Harmison, S P Jones.
Bowling: McGrath 3-1-4-0, **Lee** 4-0-19-0, **Warne** 1-0-2-0.

Day Four – Afternoon session

Trescothick became the first casualty of England's attempts to bat themselves into a winning position but fellow opener Strauss survived long enough to make his highest Ashes score.

Somerset left-hander Trescothick had enjoyed a more profitable series than his partner and his confidence was highlighted by a stylish contribution of 41 to a first-wicket stand of 64.

But for the second time in the match his demise owed more to misfortune than anything else. In the first innings his attempted sweep off Warne had bounced off the back of his bat and rolled up Gilchrist's leg straight into his gloves.

This time around he prodded down on a McGrath delivery, only to see it bounce back on to the stumps. But despite this setback the home side extended their lead at tea to 270 with eight second-innings wickets in hand after reaching 128 for two.

Strauss had survived a couple of scares before lunch but he recovered his composure after the interval to reach tea unbeaten on 57, his best effort against Australia. He got to his maiden half-century against the Australians from 89 deliveries, including five fours and a hooked six after being struck by a Lee bouncer for the second time in the match.

Vaughan was unable to repeat his first-innings century and perished in the pursuit of quick runs. His attempted hook scooped straight up to substitute fielder Brad Hodge in the deep, who claimed the catch to dismiss the England captain for 14.

New batsman Bell enjoyed some of the good fortune which had evaded Trescothick earlier in the afternoon. The Warwickshire batsman attempted to pull Lee, only for the ball to bounce on to the stumps but fail to disturb the bails.

ENGLAND: second innings
(Continued: 26-0)

M E Trescothick b McGrath	41
A J Strauss not out	57
M P Vaughan c Sub b Lee	14
I R Bell not out	8
Extras lb1 nb7	8
Total 2 wkts (35 overs)	128

Fall: 1-64 2-97.
To Bat: K P Pietersen, A Flintoff, G O Jones, A F Giles, M J Hoggard, S J Harmison, S Jones.
Bowling: McGrath 11-1-37-1, **Lee** 12-0-60 -1, **Warne** 12-2-30-0.

Day Four – Evening session

Strauss shrugged off his poor form with a sixth Test century as England finished the fourth day pressing for victory.

The Middlesex left-hander's second-innings effort of 106 off 161 was the main contribution towards setting Australia a huge chase at Old Trafford as England were able to declare on 280 for six – leaving the tourists needing 423 to win.

Strauss' struggle before tea was forgotten as he progressed towards three figures, highlighted by a pull off leg-spinner Warne into the stands to move him into the 90s. He reached his century with another similar stroke, this time for four, off McGrath as England surged towards a declaration.

Strauss, England's Man of the Series last winter in South Africa,

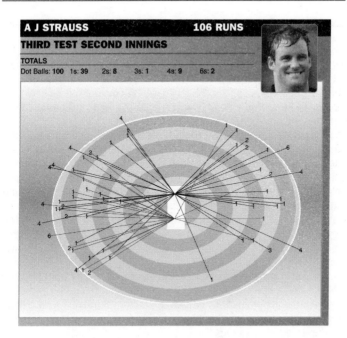

A J STRAUSS   **106 RUNS**

THIRD TEST SECOND INNINGS

TOTALS
Dot Balls: **100**   1s: **39**   2s: **8**   3s: **1**   4s: **9**   6s: **2**

was joined in a 127-run third-wicket stand with Bell, who posted his second half-century of the contest.

Ambition eventually accounted for Strauss, however, when he mis-hit another cross-bat shot off McGrath to be held in the deep by Martyn to leave England 224 for three, an overall lead of 366, though replays suggested Martyn had not taken a clean catch.

Veteran paceman McGrath claimed his 28th five-wicket haul in Tests by sending back Pietersen, Flintoff and Bell in quick succession, although he also took some punishment with Jones lofting two huge sixes to bring on a declaration from Vaughan which gave England the opportunity of 17 overs at the tourists in the remainder of the day.

That declaration ensured Australia would have to make the highest score to win a Test in history – beating the current record held by West Indies, who stacked up 418 to beat Australia two years ago in Antigua.

To put the task in perspective, however, the 231 for three

compiled by England against West Indies last year was the biggest ever successful pursuit in Manchester.

Australia closed on 24 without loss, openers Hayden and Langer surviving against the spin of Giles and Vaughan in fading light. The day's events put England firmly in the driving seat and Strauss was confident his team could bowl out Australia on the final day. 'We're not going to blow them away, but if we get the ball in the right area there's 10 wickets out there tomorrow,' he said.

On his own contribution, he added: 'It was just important we capitalised and got runs on the board, which we were able to do.

'You've got to work hard for your runs against Australia. Getting 30 and 40 really frustrated me because I'd done the hard work but they're always testing you and you know Warne is going to come on and make life difficult.

'The fact he has got me out a couple of times has made me think pretty hard about how I am looking to score off him and I have worked hard in the last couple of weeks trying to counteract his plans.

'I am better for the experience and the great thing about playing the best side in the world is you are challenged to come up with a solution to the problems they cause – if you don't find one, you will be steamrollered. It is a big thing to get a hundred against the Aussies in whatever circumstances.'

ENGLAND: second innings
(Continued: 128-2)

A J Strauss c Martyn b McGrath	106
M P Vaughan c Sub b Lee	14
I R Bell c Katich b McGrath	65
K P Pietersen lbw b McGrath	0
A Flintoff b McGrath	4
G O Jones not out	27
A F Giles not out	0

Extras b5 lb3 w1 nb14 **23**

Total 6 wkts dec (61.5 overs) **280**

Fall: 1-64, 2-97, 3-224, 4-225, 5-248, 6-264.
Did Not Bat: M J Hoggard, S J Harmison, S P Jones.
Bowling: McGrath 20.5-1-115-5, **Lee** 12-0-60-1, **Warne** 25-3-74-0, **Gillespie** 4-0-23-0.

AUSTRALIA: second innings

J L Langer not out	14
M L Hayden not out	5

Extras b4 nb1 **5**

Total 0 wkts (10 overs) **24**

To Bat: R T Ponting, D R Martyn, M J Clarke, S M Katich, A C Gilchrist, S K Warne, J N Gillespie, G D McGrath.
Bowling: Harmison 2-1-1-0, **Hoggard** 1-0-6-0, **Giles** 4-1-7-0, **Vaughan** 3-0-6-0.

Strauss displays poise and timing.

Day Five – Morning session

England were given an early boost in their hopes for victory when Hoggard made an immediate breakthrough.

Australia resumed still 399 runs away from an unlikely victory on 24 without loss but Yorkshire seamer Hoggard found the outside edge of Langer's bat with the eighth ball of the day to the delight of the 23,000 people shoehorned into Old Trafford.

Such was the expectancy surrounding England's push to go 2–1 up in the series that the gates were shut half an hour before the scheduled start time, which meant an estimated 15,000 were turned away.

The commotion outside was drowned by the celebrations for Hoggard's first success of the day, but England failed to gain a second scalp inside the first hour.

Chasing a world-record 423 for victory, Australian second-wicket pair Hayden and Ponting played their shots, while England enjoyed some good bowling conditions.

Ponting was the subject of a stumping appeal in left-arm spinner Giles' first over of the morning, but refused to be tied down by the pressure exerted.

His greeting for local hero Flintoff was emphatic, hooking a no-ball into the stands at deep square leg.

Moments later, however, Hayden edged the first of three boundaries which flew through the slips and Australia were 80 for one at drinks.

The left-hander rode his luck against the Lancashire all-rounder, playing and missing on a handful of occasions with a packed slip cordon poised. It took a change of tactic, however, to bring about his demise as Flintoff reverted to bowling over the wicket to hit leg stump, around the batsman's legs.

That strike in the 20th over of the day reduced Australia to 96 for two and gave the hosts a chance to bowl at two right-handers in Ponting and Martyn.

With a further eight overs before the interval England would have hoped to have made further inroads into Australia's batting line-up, but Ponting and Martyn shared an unbroken 25-run stand to guide them to the interval without further loss.

AUSTRALIA: second innings
(Overnight: 24-0)

J L Langer c G O Jones b Hoggard..**14**
M L Hayden b Flintoff **36**
R T Ponting not out **41**
D R Martyn not out **17**

Extras b4 nb9 **13**
Total 2 wkts (38 overs) **121**

Fall:1-25 2-96.
To Bat: M J Clarke, S M Katich, A C Gilchrist, S K Warne, J N Gillespie, G D McGrath.
Bowling: Harmison 6-1-11-0, **Hoggard** 5-0-21-1, **Giles** 14-2-41-0, **Vaughan** 3-0-6-0, **Flintoff** 7-1-30-1, **S Jones** 3-1-8-0.

Day Five – Afternoon session

Flintoff rose to the occasion in front of his home fans to lead England's pursuit of victory with two Australian wickets in the afternoon.

The Lancashire all-rounder removed Katich and the dangerous but out-of-form Gilchrist as Australia were reduced to 216 for five needing a further 207 runs to complete an unlikely victory but with a potential 40 overs still remaining in the match. The enduring feature of the day was the batting of Ponting, who was unbeaten on 91 at the interval.

The burgeoning partnership between Ponting and Martyn, which had added 25 in the morning, lasted for only another five overs in the afternoon session as England profited from a contentious decision by umpire Bucknor.

Martyn had reached 19 when he was given out lbw to Harmison despite replays showing the ball had come off the inside edge of the Australian's bat. The dismissal appeared to galvanise Ponting, who progressed to his second half-century of the series with a sequence of back-foot boundaries off Giles to help ease the pressure on his side.

While Ponting was looking extremely secure at the crease, new batsman Katich was struggling to read the reverse swing Flintoff was now beginning to utilise from the Stretford End.

Katich played and missed several times outside off stump during his 29-minute innings before he drove at a full-length ball, which flew towards the slip cordon and Giles claimed a catch to his right at wide third slip to dismiss the batsman for 12.

Flintoff struck again eight overs later to end Gilchrist's struggle at the crease – he had scored only 4 off 30 balls – when once again he drove at a full-length ball but edged straight to Bell in the gully. It was just reward for the inspirational England all-rounder, whose superb spell included a burst of two for 6 in 29 balls.

That breakthrough brought Clarke to the crease, now recovered from the back trouble that had plagued him throughout the Test, and he successfully reached 20 by the interval with Ponting looking set for the whole day.

AUSTRALIA: second innings
(Continued: 121-2)

M L Hayden b Flintoff **36**
R T Ponting not out **91**
D R Martyn lbw b Harmison **19**
S M Katich c Giles b Flintoff **12**
A C Gilchrist c Bell b Flintoff **4**
M J Clarke not out **20**

Extras b4 w1 nb15 **20**
Total 5 wkts (66 overs) **216**

Fall: 1-25 2-96 3-129 4-165 5-182
To Bat: S K Warne, J N Gillespie, G D McGrath.
Bowling: Harmison 12-3-27-1, **Hoggard** 7-1-26-1, **Giles**
20-2-68-0, **Vaughan** 5-0-21-0, **Flintoff** 15- 3-50-3, **S Jones**
7-2-20-0.

Day Five – Evening session

England narrowly failed to claim a major advantage in the Ashes series after Australia clung on to claim a draw in another tense and dramatic finish.

Just eight days after holding their nerve to claim a 2-run triumph to level the series at Edgbaston, England this time failed by one wicket to claim the victory that would have secured a 2–1 lead in the series with two Tests remaining.

Roared on by a capacity crowd, England were unable to break the last-wicket partnership between Lee and McGrath with the former hitting the last ball of the match from Harmison for four to reach an unbeaten 18 as Australia finished on 371 for nine – 52 short of a record-breaking victory.

The hero of the day was Ponting, who responded to yet another crisis in Australia's top order with a brilliant 156, the 23rd century of his Test career and his fifth in Ashes cricket.

Ponting's disciplined innings, forged over nearly seven hours at the crease and including a six and 16 fours, was the model of restraint and provided almost single-handed resistance to another barrage of hostility from England's seamers as they looked for victory. He completed his century shortly after tea and shared a crucial 81-run partnership with Clarke which ate up valuable overs and time.

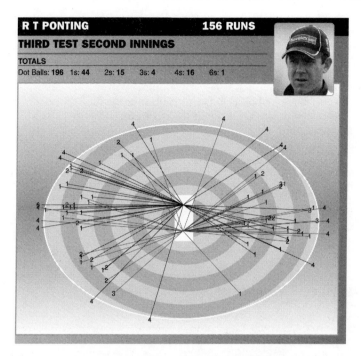

R T PONTING   **156 RUNS**

THIRD TEST SECOND INNINGS

TOTALS

Dot Balls: **196**   1s: **44**   2s: **15**   3s: **4**   4s: **16**   6s: **1**

Jones, fast becoming England's talisman during this series, ended Clarke's resistance with a superb inswinger which took out his off stump and Australia's strange decision to promote Gillespie up the order was quickly halted when he was trapped leg before in the next over.

As England's supporters celebrated what seemed like an inevitable victory, once again they came up against a major stumbling block in Warne and his irritating ability to occupy the crease.

Warne scored 34 but kept Ponting company at the crease for 22 crucial overs after England missed a major chance to secure the priceless victory. Australia's legendary leg-spinner had progressed to 30 when he clipped Jones off his legs straight to Pietersen at midwicket, who spilled his fifth catch of the series and allowed Warne to bat for an extra half an hour.

That looked like England's final chance at snatching victory until the return of Flintoff for one final spell, this time from the Brian

Statham End. From there he ended Warne's resistance when he edged to Strauss at second slip, who palmed the ball away to allow wicketkeeper Jones to take a diving catch.

England's confidence in an imminent victory was lifted further when Ponting was finally dismissed five overs later after gloving Harmison behind, but they were unable to break Australia's determined resistance as the tension grew in the final four overs.

After securing a remarkable draw, Ponting admitted he thought the game might have been lost after he was dismissed late in the day.

'Having worked as hard as I had, I was trying to take as much strike as I could. I thought the game might have slipped away but full credit to Brett and Glenn, they did what they had to do,' he said.

'We did not have a realistic chance of winning here but it was a tough day's Test cricket that we had to play and we have done it.'

Match drawn
AUSTRALIA: second innings
(Continued: 216-5)

J L Langer c G O Jones b Hoggard	14
M L Hayden b Flintoff	36
R T Ponting c G O Jones b Harmison	156
D R Martyn lbw b Harmison	19
S M Katich c Giles b Flintoff	12
A C Gilchrist c Bell b Flintoff	4
M J Clarke b S P Jones	39
J N Gillespie lbw b Hoggard	0
S K Warne c G O Jones b Flintoff	34
B Lee not out	18
G D McGrath not out	5

Extras b5 lb8 w2 nb19 **34**
Total 9 wkts (108 overs) **371**
Fall: 1-25, 2-96, 3-129, 4-165, 5-182, 6-263, 7-264, 8-340, 9-354.
Bowling: Harmison 22-4-67-2, **Hoggard** 13-0-49-2, **Giles** 26-4-93-0, **Vaughan** 5-0-21-0, **Flintoff** 25-6-71-4, **S Jones** 17-3-57-1.

Warne enjoyed one of his most prosperous series with the bat, but a Test century is still elusive.

Man of the match – Ricky Ponting

For Ponting, captaining Australia was the easiest job he ever had in cricket. With McGrath and Warne mainstays in his team and Australia dominating world cricket, all he had to do was send out his players with the instructions to carry on doing what they were good at.

But if ever he had to earn his money it was at Old Trafford. Reeling from the defeat at Edgbaston, he found himself in the unfamiliar position of staring at a huge target with England scenting victory.

What followed was an absolute masterclass in concentration and determination for almost seven hours. With wickets tumbling around him, Ponting accepted that, as captain, he had to take responsibility for saving the match. His innings was more remarkable as in five previous knocks he had reached double figures only twice, with just one half-century.

Ponting drew on all his reserves to keep the England attack at bay. There are only a handful of batsmen who could have played a similar innings and, in the context of the game, the series and the criticism he was facing over his captaincy, it was a brilliant piece of disciplined batting.

Ponting at Old Trafford

Batting: ....7 and 156

Fourth Test Day One – Morning session

Trescothick spearheaded England's bright start to the crucial fourth Ashes Test, exploiting Australia's under-strength attack to claim a half-century on the opening morning at Trent Bridge.

The Somerset left-hander, still awaiting his first Ashes century in his 14th Test against Australia, seized on the absence of injured McGrath to dominate the opening session and guide England to 129 for one at lunch.

Trescothick hit an unbeaten 62 – which included eight fours and a six, hit down the ground off Warne – and ensured England continued their momentum after stunning displays in the previous Tests at Edgbaston and Old Trafford.

England's hopes of taking control of the series were lifted even before the start when McGrath, who had expected to shrug off a right elbow problem, failed his fitness test, forcing Australia to recall Michael Kasprowicz to their line-up. The disappointing Jason Gillespie made way for 22-year-old debutant Shaun Tait.

Without McGrath, Australia struggled to maintain a tight line and length and delivered 14 no-balls in their first 20 overs – with Kasprowicz the main culprit, over-stepping seven times in his eight-over new-ball burst.

That poor discipline enabled England to battle through a cautious start and impose themselves on Australia's attack with a 105-run opening stand.

Trescothick had taken 21 balls to get off the mark when he clipped Lee off his legs for four to begin England's onslaught, with opening partner Strauss soon hitting Kasprowicz for successive boundaries.

Tait struggled for direction during his opening five-over spell – with Trescothick square-driving successive boundaries. Ponting introduced Warne's guile in the 18th over, but he was treated with little respect by Trescothick who launched him down the ground for six in his second over to help him to a half-century.

Strauss looked set to follow him to the landmark but fell for 35 in Warne's third over, getting a bottom edge on to his boot as he tried a sweep, and the ball looped up to Hayden at slip. Vaughan got off the mark to the very next ball, cutting Warne for four, while Trescothick became the major beneficiary of Australia's no-ball problem when he chopped Lee on to his stumps – only to be reprieved by umpire Aleem Dar's signal. Straightaway he seized on his second chance by pulling the next delivery, which was also called for a no-ball, for four.

ENGLAND: first innings

M E Trescothick not out...62
A J Strauss c Hayden b Warne 35
M P Vaughan not out...14
                                                          Extras nb18 **18**
                                        Total 1 wkt (27 overs) **129**
Fall: 1-105.
To Bat: I R Bell, K P Pietersen, A Flintoff, G O Jones, A F Giles,
M J Hoggard, S J Harmison, S P Jones.
Bowling: Lee 9-1-44-0, **Kasprowicz** 8-1-37-0, **Tait** 5-0-26-0,
Warne 5-1-22-1.

Day One – Afternoon session

England would have wanted to capitalise on the positive start in the morning session, but their progress was held up immediately after lunch as the first of the showers forecast for the day turned up.

With the first downpour ceasing within an hour, however, umpires Dar and Steve Bucknor decided play could resume at 2.10 p.m.

But only 12 minutes of action were possible as more wet weather blew in. Rookie Tait sent down a testing maiden to Vaughan among the 20 balls bowled, but England were then forced off once again with the score on 134 for one.

Once the showers ceased the umpires made a further inspection and decided to take an early tea at 3.10 p.m. with a view to restarting 20 minutes later. That time was then put back by 25 minutes after yet more rain.

ENGLAND: first innings
(Continued: 129-1)

M E Trescothick not out 65
A J Strauss c Hayden b Warne 35
M P Vaughan not out 15
                                                          Extras nb19 **19**
                                        Total 1 wkt (30.1 overs) **134**
Fall: 1-105.
To Bat: I R Bell, K P Pietersen, A Flintoff, G O Jones, A F Giles,
M J Hoggard, S P Harmison, S P Jones.
Bowling: Lee 9-1-44-0, **Kasprowicz** 10-1-42-0, **Tait** 6.1-1-26-0,
Warne 5-1-22-1.

Day One – Evening session

England's desire to make a statement of intent and undermine Australia's fragile morale backfired as the tourists battled back impressively from an uncertain start to restrict their hosts to 229 for four.

The rain disruption had allowed Australia to regroup and when they resumed, with England 134 for one, they made the final session count.

Trescothick, who had sat in the pavilion for a long time on 65 thinking about his maiden Ashes century, was not given the chance to get a start as he fell to the fourth ball after the resumption. He was Tait's first Test victim – losing his middle stump to an inswinging delivery.

Tait, whose slingshot delivery had been timed at 93.5 mph earlier in the day, claimed his second wicket for 8 runs in nine balls when Bell pushed tentatively forward to an outswinger and edged behind to Gilchrist to leave England on 146 for three.

With ideal overhead conditions for swing bowlers, the advantage seemed to have shifted back towards Australia – but not for the first time in the series they squandered two further opportunities in the next seven overs.

Pietersen, at a venue where he played his first four seasons of county cricket, had only 14 to his name when he provided Australia with their first chance, Kasprowicz missing a sharp caught and bowled opportunity. Pietersen progressed to an unbeaten 33 by the close, but fortunately for Australia their miss off Vaughan was not as expensive as it could have been. The England captain had reached a battling 30 when he also attempted to be positive against Kasprowicz and drove off the back foot, only to be dropped by Hayden in the gully.

For a further 14 overs, Hayden must have wondered if he had gifted England a chance to reclaim the Ashes as Vaughan teamed up with Pietersen in a profitable 67-run stand which seemed to be regaining England's momentum.

Ponting, who had only four previous victims in 92 Tests, was so desperate for the breakthrough that he decided to introduce his own medium pace. The change worked a treat, Ponting worrying England's batsmen into defensive submission – both of them afraid of the ignominy of being dismissed by such a part-time bowler – and then nicking a wicket.

Pietersen was fortunate not to be run out off Ponting's third ball when he scrambled down the pitch for a single from the non-striker's end only to be sent back by Vaughan. He would have been several feet short of his ground had Hayden's throw hit the stumps.

As it was, Ponting instead claimed the scalp of Vaughan, who pushed nervously outside off stump and edged behind to Gilchrist only four overs before the premature finish for rain.

It left England's two big hitters, Pietersen and Flintoff, facing the

Rookie Tait gets in on the action. Ian Bell departs for just 3.

task of rebuilding on Friday, a crucial period according to Trescothick.

'We have just got our noses in front. The morning session is crucial in the context of our first innings and maybe in the context of the game: if we bat well through to lunch we will be looking at a good score, if we lose a couple of wickets we will have to battle as long as we can,' he said.

'The way this series has been, you are never really miles ahead, they keep nagging away and asking questions at the right time.'

Debutant Tait was the pick of the bowlers after his slow start, finishing the day with two for 62.

'The guys talked to me about the best moments in your first game: the presentation of the baggy green cap and your first wicket,' said the 22-year-old.

'The wicket was the better feeling. I was a little bit nervous and being uptight meant I did not let myself go as much as I should have. I bowled better after that.'

ENGLAND: first innings
(Continued: 134-1)

M E Trescothick b Tait	**65**
A J Strauss c Hayden b Warne	**35**
M P Vaughan c Gilchrist b Ponting	**58**
I R Bell c Gilchrist b Tait	**3**
K P Pietersen not out	**33**
A Flintoff not out	**8**

Extras lb4 w1 nb22 **7**
Total 4 wkts (60 overs) **229**

Fall: 1-105　2-137　3-146　4-213.
To Bat: G O Jones, A F Giles, M J Hoggard, S J Harmison, S Jones.
Bowling: Lee 16-1-75-0, **Kasprowicz** 18-2-56-0, **Tait** 14-1-62-2, **Warne** 6-1-23-1, **Ponting** 6-2-9-1.

Day Two – Morning session

Flintoff dominated another crucial century partnership with Geraint Jones to lift England towards a major first-innings total.

The Lancashire all-rounder hammered an unbeaten 73 and teamed up with Jones in an 103-run sixth-wicket partnership, their fourth century stand together.

The pair helped England recover to reach 344 for five after the early loss of Pietersen. Resuming on 229 for four, hoping to reach 400, England's hopes suffered an early setback with Pietersen falling to the 25th ball of the morning, delivered by fast bowler Lee.

Pietersen, hoping to claim his maiden Test century at the ground where he played with Nottinghamshire, had progressed from 33 overnight to reach 45 when Lee delivered a full-length outswinger which he edged behind to wicketkeeper Gilchrist.

That reunited Flintoff and Jones, who quickly set about taking the attack to Australia and dominated the remainder of the morning session after battling through the tricky early stages of their partnership.

Flintoff had not added to his overnight 8 when he survived a loud appeal from Warne for lbw after taking a big stride down the wicket. He also got away with a wild back-foot slash over the slips off Lee, but it took another drive down the ground off Warne, stepping down the wicket to hit him over the top, to get back into his stride.

Kasprowicz almost broke the partnership when Flintoff, who had progressed to 24, he nibbled down the leg side and saw the ball narrowly evaded Gilchrist's dive. But after those nervous early stages, he grew in confidence and contributed 64 to a century stand off only 126 balls, having already brought up his third half-century of the series by sweeping Warne for six.

Jones wisely played a supportive role to Flintoff's big hitting but was able to claim two cover boundaries off Lee and rotated the strike impressively as Australia strived unsuccessfully for a breakthrough.

Even Australia's decision to take the new ball failed to stop England's momentum, with Tait conceding 21 runs in three overs while Flintoff hit four fours in six balls. Flintoff reached the interval having hit a six and 11 fours during his thrilling 94-ball innings and had helped England add 115 precious runs in the 29 overs of the morning session while Jones was unbeaten on 34.

ENGLAND: first innings
(Continued: 229-4)

K P Pietersen c Gilchrist b Lee	**45**
A Flintoff not out	73
G O Jones not out	34
Extras lb6 w1 nb24	**31**
Total 5 wkts (89 overs)	**344**

Fall: 1-105 2-137 3-146 4-213 5-241.
To Bat: A F Giles, M J Hoggard, S J Harmison, S P Jones.
Bowling: Lee 25-1-106-1, **Kasprowicz** 25-3-78-0, **Tait** 17-1-83-2, **Warne** 16-1-62-1, **Ponting** 6-2-9-1.

Day Two – Afternoon session

Flintoff continued his display of destructive strokeplay to complete his maiden Ashes century as England amassed a commanding first-innings total.

He scored a stunning 102, hammering a six and 14 fours during his 132-ball innings, dominating a 177-run sixth-wicket stand with Geraint Jones which helped the hosts reach 477 all out at tea.

Jones played a supporting role for the majority of the partnership but opened up after the Lancastrian's demise to score 85, his highest score of the series.

Having dominated the bowling in the morning the onslaught continued after the interval, although Jones survived a close appeal for a catch behind on 34 to the first delivery after lunch, with Lee convinced he had given a thin edge behind.

Those narrow escapes did not affect England's appetite for runs, though, and they added 73 from the first 14 overs with the new ball – a rate which was only halted as Flintoff approached the century mark.

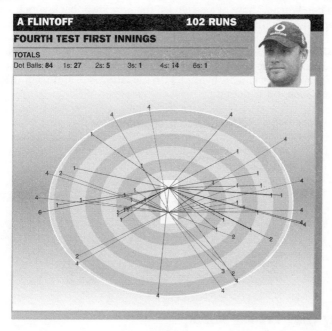

A FLINTOFF   **102 RUNS**

FOURTH TEST FIRST INNINGS

TOTALS

Dot Balls: **84**   1s: **27**   2s: **5**   3s: **1**   4s: **14**   6s: **1**

Having flayed Australia's attack all around Trent Bridge he finally began to show signs of nerves when he reached 99, and stayed 1 run short of the landmark for 10 minutes before finally claiming the single off Warne which clinched his fifth Test ton. He celebrated in subdued fashion, raising his bat to all corners of the 15,500-capacity ground.

His century came up from 121 deliveries, which included 14 fours and a mighty six off the leg-spinner. Just three overs later Flintoff was awarded another standing ovation, but this time it was to mark the end of his innings.

Tait won an lbw appeal when Flintoff aimed a blow to leg and was pinned on the pads, having added only 2 more to his ton.

It ended a stand of 177 and sparked a collapse as England lost five wickets for 59 runs in 19 overs, missing out on an opportunity to score 500 against Australia for the first time since Perth in 1986.

Jones offered a return catch off a mistimed drive to Kasprowicz nine overs later having helped post 450, departing just 15 short of a deserved century himself.

Then Warne, showing no signs of the sore lower back which had been troubling him, wrapped up with the tail to finish with four for 102 – including two wickets in a seven-ball spell.

Giles made 15 before he was trapped leg before, while Hoggard and Harmison both succumbed to the Warne–Gilchrist double act; the former being caught behind with the latter well stumped. It left Simon Jones on 15 not out.

ENGLAND: first innings
(Continued: 344-5)

M E Trescothick b Tait...**65**
A J Strauss c Hayden b Warne **35**
M P Vaughan c Gilchrist b Ponting **58**
I R Bell c Gilchrist b Tait **3**
K P Pietersen c Gilchrist b Lee **45**
A Flintoff lbw b Tait...**102**
G O Jones c & b Kasprowicz..**85**
A F Giles lbw b Warne..**15**
M J Hoggard c Gilchrist b Warne..**10**
S J Harmison st Gilchrist b Warne..**2**
S Jones not out **15**
Extras b1 lb15 w1 nb25 **42**
Total (123.1 overs) **477**
Fall: 1-105, 2-137, 3-146, 4-213, 5-241, 6-418, 7-450, 8-450, 9-454.
Bowling: Lee 32-2-131-1, **Kasprowicz** 32-3-122-1, **Tait** 24-4-97-3, **Warne** 29.1-4-102-4, **Ponting** 6-2-9-1.

Day Two – Evening session

A devastating spell of bowling from Hoggard built on the foundations laid down by Flintoff's maiden Ashes hundred as England extended their domination to the end of the second day by reducing Australia to 99 for five at stumps.

Yorkshire swing bowler Hoggard exploited the overhead conditions perfectly as his 11-over spell from the Radcliffe Road end reaped figures of three for 32.

With Simon Jones and Harmison picking up a wicket apiece, the tourists found themselves trailing by 378 and under massive pressure. Opener Hayden survived when an inside edge saved him from a huge shout for lbw in the 10th over, Hoggard's fifth. But it was the briefest of reprieves as the very next delivery swung back in to leave umpire Dar in no doubt.

Welshman Jones followed up with one which nipped back to Ponting, who played around the ball, and watched as West Indian Bucknor raised the finger in typical time-freezing style. Hoggard made it three for 2 in 11 balls when an off-cutter sneaked past the inside edge of Damien Martyn's bat.

Left-hander Langer dug in alongside Michael Clarke but was roughed up by a Flintoff bouncer that struck him on the helmet. Moments later he jabbed a ball from Hoggard into his pads and perished as Bell dived forward to hold the catch at short leg, the batsman departing for 27.

Harmison ensured England left the field to a standing ovation by claiming a fourth leg before decision to remove Clarke for 36 and signal the end of play.

Australia vice-captain Gilchrist conceded his team were not accustomed to the situation they had found themselves in but stressed they had to counter-attack if they were not to slip 2–1 behind with one to play.

'England are doing to us what we have done to other teams over a number of years,' said Gilchrist.

'We haven't come out of it very well so far, we have hung in there and again we are under pressure. Mentally it is a different area for us to be in and that is pretty taxing, but we will keep fighting.

'We certainly didn't underestimate England. But they have continued to show the world, not just us, that they are a very good and very dangerous cricket team at the top of their game.'

Hoggard is often the England bowler who receives the least public acclaim, but Flintoff said the Yorkshireman fully deserved the plaudits after his late spell.

'We have different bowlers for different conditions and this one suited Hoggy more than the others. The ball has swung and he's put it in the right areas,' he said.

'Different people get wickets at different times and I think that's the good thing about the bowling attack – we bowl for each other and we're happy with each others' success.

'One of the good things about this side and what's made us successful is different people sticking their hand up when it's needed.'

AUSTRALIA: first innings

J L Langer c Bell b Hoggard	27
M L Hayden lbw b Hoggard	7
R T Ponting lbw b S P Jones	1
D R Martyn lbw b Hoggard	1
M J Clarke lbw b Harmison	36
S M Katich not out	20

Extras lb1 nb6 **7**
Total 5 wkts (30.3 overs) **99**

Fall: 1-20 2-21 3-22 4-58 5-99.
To Bat: A C Gilchrist, S K Warne, S W Tait, M S Kasprowicz.
Bowling: Harmison 5.3-1-25-1, **Hoggard** 11-3-32-3, **S Jones** 9-3-22-1, **Flintoff** 5-0-19-0.

Day Three – Morning session

Simon Jones blasted through the Australian batting on the morning of the third day as England hastened their chase of Ashes success.

Welshman Jones struck twice in as many balls and finished with a five-wicket haul to ensure Vaughan's men forced home the initiative gained by scoring 477 on the opening day.

Then, after Flintoff undid Gilchrist for the fourth time in the series thanks to a stunning catch from Strauss, Jones finished off the innings for 218 with two more to register figures of five for 44.

After a brief consultation with his players before they left the field, England captain Vaughan decided to enforce the follow-on – the first time Australia had been asked to do so since September 1988 against Pakistan. In their second innings they reached 14 without loss at lunch.

It had appeared England would have a tough task to close the Australian first innings as Australian pair Katich and Gilchrist rattled along at a run a ball for the opening three-quarters of an hour.

The pair were flinging the bat and, although they were often getting beaten outside off stump, they refused to let that faze them as they combated the swing on offer by committing to full-blooded strokes.

Hoggard, England's hero the previous evening with three wickets, bore the brunt of the assault with his third over costing 22, including a huge six from Gilchrist into the stand at the Radcliffe Road end. In all, 41 runs came from three overs, with even Flintoff suffering.

Simon Jones' ability to reverse-swing the ball at high pace was central to England's plans.

However, the introduction of Jones from the Radcliffe Road End produced immediate dividends. He made his mark with just his second delivery when Katich flashed a wide half-volley to Strauss at gully.

Having halted that 58-run stand, Jones then sent back Warne – so often the major irritant to England's bowlers in this series – when a leading edge looped to Bell at cover.

The double blow signalled something of a change in tempo, quelling what had been a brilliant Australian counter-attack. Flintoff followed up by finding the edge of Gilchrist's bat, and Strauss took what was arguably the catch of the summer.

Strauss, in the slips, took off to his left to hold on and ensure Gilchrist's run without a half-century continued. The England fielder was at full stretch, body horizontal, when he completed the catch. Jones then conjured up an outswinger which proved far too good for former Glamorgan team-mate Kasprowicz, beating the outside edge and hitting off stump after starting down the leg side.

But Lee refused to go down without a fight, clubbing Harmison right out of the ground on two occasions and hitting another six through his favourite midwicket area off Jones during a daring 47. His luck ran out, however, when he upper-cut Jones to third man where Bell claimed the catch that ended the innings. England were afforded four overs at the Australians second time around before lunch but could not add to their good morning's work. Influenced by the aerial movement on offer, Vaughan turned to Hoggard and Jones immediately.

Yorkshire's Hoggard did find the edge of Langer's bat from the second delivery of the innings but the ball flew through a vacant fourth slip area and the Aussies reached the interval without loss.

AUSTRALIA: first innings
(Continued: 99-5)

S M Katich c Strauss b S Jones 45
A C Gilchrist c Strauss b Flintoff 27
S K Warne c Bell b S Jones 0
B Lee c Bell b S P Jones..47
M S Kasprowicz b S Jones 5
S W Tait not out..3

Extras lb2 w1 nb16 **19**
Total (49.1 overs) **218**

Fall: 1-20, 2-21, 3-22, 4-58, 5-99, 6-157, 7-157, 8-163, 9-175.
Bowling: Harmison 9-1-48-1, **Hoggard** 15-3-70-3, **S Jones** 14.1-4-44-5, **Flintoff** 11-1-54-1.

AUSTRALIA: second innings

J L Langer not out 9
M L Hayden not out 5

Total 0 wkts (4 overs) **14**

To Bat: R T Ponting, D R Martyn, S M Katich, M J Clarke, A C Gilchrist, S K Warne, S W Tait, M S Kasprowicz.
Bowling: Hoggard 2-1-6-0, **S Jones** 2-0-8-0.

Day Three – Afternoon session

After the heroics of the morning, England were handicapped by an injury to bowling hero Simon Jones. They found Australia harder to break down as the tourists reached 115 for one.

Having seized on the opportunity to become the first side in 191 Tests to enforce the follow-on against Australia, England struggled to make the same inroads second time around when their opponents resumed after lunch 245 runs adrift with all 10 second innings wickets in hand.

The loss of Jones was a major blow, especially as he had been the most potent bowler in the morning session, taking four wickets before lunch.

He complained of a sore right ankle, and was taken to hospital for a scan on the area having left the field shortly after lunch.

England had to wait 14 overs before making a breakthrough as Langer and Hayden shared a 50-run opening stand. Unsurprisingly it was England's Man of the Series Flintoff who finally separated the pair. With his fourth ball from the Pavilion End he tempted Hayden, who had made 26, into driving loosely at a full-length ball outside off stump and Giles claimed the catch at wide fourth slip.

The Lancashire all-rounder could also have claimed a second victim eight overs later with opener Langer edging a regulation catch to Strauss at second slip, but this time he put it down. Langer was 37 at the time and exploited his reprieve by progressing to his second half-century of the series by tea while captain Ponting had reached an unbeaten 28 to frustrate England's hopes of making further inroads.

```
J L Langer not out ....................................................................54
M L Hayden c Giles b Flintoff  ..................................................26
R T Ponting not out ...................................................................28
                                         Extras b1 lb2 nb4 7
                                    Total 1 wkt (31 overs) 115
Fall: 1-50.
To Bat: D R Martyn, S M Katich, M J Clarke, A C Gilchrist, S K
Warne, S W Tait, M S Kasprowicz.
Bowling: Hoggard 7-2-25-0, S Jones 4-0-15-0, Harmison
11-1-44-0, Flintoff 7-2-23-1, Giles 2-0-5-0.
```

Day Three – Evening session

Flintoff starred once again late on for England, stepping into the vacancy left by injured fellow paceman Simon Jones to edge his side nearer to a victory at Trent Bridge.

With Jones off the field with an injured ankle, the bowling responsibilities had to be shared out between the three quicks, and typically Flintoff was not one to shy away from the challenge.

His introduction at the Radcliffe Road End was the catalyst for two wickets within minutes of each other, disrupting an Australian side which had been looking quite comfortable at 155 for two.

The first ball of a new spell resulted in the spectacular run-out of Australia's captain Ponting, which in itself sparked off controversy. The Australia captain fell 2 runs short of a half-century when substitute Gary Pratt effected a direct hit from cover after Martyn pushed forward to Flintoff and called for a single.

Australia had been concerned by England's regular employment of the 12th man throughout the entire tour especially as they chose to use specialist fielders rather than the one player in the original match squad who had been left out. The unlucky man, usually Tremlett of Hampshire, would return to county cricket duty.

Ponting expressed his displeasure to Vaughan's team as they huddled in celebration at the fall of the wicket and he then appeared to say something to England coach Duncan Fletcher on the home balcony as he departed for 48 after television replays confirmed his dismissal by one of domestic cricket's best fielders. If Ponting's departure was not bad enough, Martyn then flirted outside off stump to give Flintoff his second success of the innings as wicketkeeper Geraint Jones claimed the catch.

Australia were indebted to an unbroken partnership between Clarke and Katich which took them to 222 for four by the time bad light allowed them some respite with 10 overs still left to bowl.

At the end of play Ponting – who was later fined 75 per cent of his match fee by International Cricket Council match referee Ranjan Madugalle – made a public apology for his heated outburst as tensions boiled over with his side under pressure and still 37 runs behind.

'I am very disappointed with my dismissal given that it was at a crucial stage of the game and I had worked really hard to get to that position,' he said. 'I no doubt let myself down with my reaction and for that I apologise to those that view me as a role model.

'My frustration at getting out was compounded by the fact that I was run out by a substitute fielder – an issue which has concerned us from the start of this series and one we raised prior to this series.'

Fletcher claimed he could not hear what Ponting had to say due to 'the crowd going ballistic at that stage'. But he defended England's policy of allowing their bowling attack to rehydrate while substituting them with young, agile replacements.

'We try to get someone who is not playing first-class cricket, usually from a county who are having a rest,' said Fletcher.

'We have had Gary around as 12th man on numerous occasions. In the modern game you have to take on a lot of fluids: at some stage you have to come off to relieve yourself of those fluids.

'It was brought up during the one-day series but nothing was said by the match referee. We just leave it to the referee and the umpires.'

Langer explained Australia's frustration that the series hosts had cottoned on to the idea before them.

'In cricket there are great traditions, particularly in Test cricket,' he said. 'As long as I have played the game the 12th man is usually one of the bowlers. But Englishmen are much more intelligent than Australians – you only have to look at the Barmy Army – and therefore it's no surprise they have come up with this before us.

'Perhaps in this day of professionalism it is just the best way of getting the best out of the resources available – everyone is looking to find the edge.'

AUSTRALIA: second innings
(Continued: 14-0)

J L Langer c Bell b Giles	61
M L Hayden c Giles b Flintoff	26
R T Ponting run out	48
D R Martyn c G O Jones b Flintoff	13
M J Clarke not out	39
S M Katich not out	24

Extras b1 lb2 nb8 **11**
Total 4 wkts (67 overs) **222**

Fall: 1-50, 2-129, 3-155, 4-161.
To Bat: A C Gilchrist, S K Warne, S W Tait, M S Kasprowicz.
Bowling: Hoggard 15-5-44-0, **S Jones** 4-0-15-0, **Harmison** 15-2-54-0, **Flintoff** 13-3-33-2, **Giles** 17-1-62-1, **Bell** 3-0-11-0.

Day Four – Morning session

Hoggard made an important breakthrough for England as they attempted to force victory in the fourth Test after Australia's stubborn batting had frustrated them for most of the fourth morning.

Resuming 37 runs adrift on 222 for four having been forced to follow on, Australia batted cautiously but effectively to wipe out the deficit with Clarke and Katich forging a century partnership.

But just one over before lunch Clarke edged Yorkshire seamer Hoggard behind to Geraint Jones for 56 as Australia reached 270 for five at the interval, finally ahead by 11 runs but needing to establish a much larger lead if they were to avoid falling 2–1 behind in the series.

England had hoped Simon Jones would have recovered sufficiently to play his part in helping in the victory push, but after treatment overnight he was still deemed unfit to take the field at the start.

It left England with only four full-time bowlers – Harmison, Flintoff, Hoggard and Giles – to try to dismiss Australia.

The tourists exploited Jones' absence, as Clarke and Katich frustrated England for 29 overs with relatively few alarms.

England's only chance of a breakthrough came in the sixth over of the day when Clarke, given a reprieve the previous evening after wicketkeeper Geraint Jones fluffed a stumping when he had scored 35, edged Giles but silly mid-off Bell failed to take the low catch.

Clarke recovered from that early escape to reach his half-century, but it was not until the 19th over of the morning that he registered Australia's first boundary of the day, edging Hoggard to third man for four.

Clarke then edged between wicketkeeper Jones and Trescothick off Ashley Giles, bowling the 75th over of the innings.

He endured a scare two overs later when he set off for a single only to be sent back by Katich, just getting back as Giles' throw whizzed past the stumps at the bowler's end. Clarke's disciplined approach finally deserted him on 56 when he nudged at a delivery outside off stump and edged behind to grateful wicketkeeper Jones to end a stand of exactly 100.

Gilchrist started in predictable fashion and drove two boundaries before lunch while Katich progressed to 41 after over three hours of defiance.

AUSTRALIA: second innings
(Overnight: 222-4)

M J Clarke c G O Jones b Hoggard	56
S M Katich not out	41
A C Gilchrist not out	9
Extras b1 lb4 nb11	16
Total 5 wkts (96 overs)	270

Fall: 1-50, 2-129, 3-155, 4-161, 5-261.
To Bat: S K Warne, S W Tait, M S Kasprowicz.
Bowling: Hoggard 21-7-53-1, **S Jones** 4-0-15-0, **Harmison** 21-3-64-0, Flintoff 21-4-50-2, Giles 23-3-71-1, Bell 6-2-12-0.

Day Four – Afternoon session

Resuming at 270 for five with Katich 41 not out, the Australian resistance crumbled and they lost four wickets for 73 runs with only Katich – who battled for 261 minutes to reach 59 – showing any sustained resistance.

Any hopes of the tail holding out to salvage a draw proved futile as three wickets fell in 14 overs.

Adam Gilchrist (11) was first to go in the afternoon when he fell lbw to Hoggard. Then Katich became the latest victim of a suspect umpiring decision.

Katich had scored only four boundaries during a long spell of defiance and looked bemused when umpire Dar raised his finger to a Harmison delivery which hit the batsman on the flap of a pad and appeared to be bouncing over the stumps.

Warne lifted Australian spirits by hammering 45 off 42 balls, including two sixes and five fours, but was stumped by Geraint Jones after advancing down the wicket to try to hit Giles for his second six of the over.

Seven overs later Harmison claimed his second wicket of the innings with Kasprowicz getting a thin edge behind to wicketkeeper Geraint Jones. Kasprowicz had been dropped at midwicket in the previous over by Pietersen, his sixth missed catch of the series.

Harmison eventually finished off the innings by bowling last man Tait who, with defence a priority, showed his inexperience by attempting a one-day shot, stepping outside off stump to try to exploit the gaps on the on side.

England closed in on a key triumph after dismissing Australia for 387, leaving them to chase a victory target of just 129 in the final session.

AUSTRALIA: second innings
(Continued: 270-5)

J L Langer c Bell b Giles	61
M L Hayden c Giles b Flintoff	26
R T Ponting run out	48
D R Martyn c G O Jones b Flintoff	13
M J Clarke c G O Jones b Hoggard	56
S M Katich lbw b Harmison	59
A C Gilchrist lbw b Hoggard	11
S K Warne st G O Jones b Giles	45
B Lee not out	26
M S Kasprowicz c G O Jones b Harmison	19
S W Tait b Harmison	4

Extras b1 lb4 nb14 **19**
Total (124 overs) **387**

Fall:1-50 2-129 3-155 4-161 5-261 6-277 7-314 8-342 9-373
Bowling: Hoggard 27-7-72-2, **S Jones** 4-0-15-0, **Harmison** 30-5-93-3, **Flintoff** 29-4-83-2, **Giles** 28-3-107-2, **Bell** 6-2-12-0.

Day Four – Evening session

England's Ashes dream moved a step closer to reality as they held their nerve in another thrilling finish to edge a three-wicket victory and claim a crucial 2–1 lead heading into the final Test.

Chasing a modest 129 runs for victory, England's task seemed straightforward until Warne was introduced in the sixth over and immediately sparked panic among the ranks.

Warne claimed three for 7 in 29 balls to leave England reeling on 57 for four and, despite Pietersen and Flintoff adding a priceless 46 runs, it took a brave eighth-wicket stand between Giles and Hoggard to clinch victory.

It was not until Giles pushed Warne through the on side to score the winning runs shortly before 6.30 p.m. that England's victory was confirmed.

Another capacity crowd had expected to witness a relaxed and comfortable progress towards the win – in stark contrast to the previous two Tests, when England narrowly clinched victory at Edgbaston and came within one wicket of winning at Old Trafford.

But for the third time in the series these two sides conjured up another emotional roller-coaster of a finish.

England ensured Australia could not win the series, but the Aussies could still retain the Ashes if they bounced back from another close defeat to win at the Oval and draw the series 2–2.

This triumph was a tribute to the collective will of England's vibrant side and, unlike Headingley in 1981 when Australia memorably failed by 18 runs to chase down a victory target of 130, the hosts finally overcame their nerves with Giles and Hoggard combining to add the final 13 runs required for victory.

Trescothick led the charge by hitting 27 off 22 balls, exploiting two wayward overs from Kasprowicz with the new ball, but the introduction of Warne as his replacement in the attack changed the mood of the match.

Warne struck with his first ball with Trescothick pushing forward defensively and edging low to captain Ponting at silly point. The leg-spinner followed that by removing Vaughan with the first ball of his next over, this time inducing an edge to Hayden at slip.

By the time Warne also dismissed Strauss (23), to a low catch at leg slip which needed a referral to third umpire Mark Benson to clarify, England's nerve was beginning to fray at 57 for three. That was underlined by Bell's ill-timed decision to pull Lee straight to the

Probably the most important runs Ashley Giles will ever score.

safe hands of Kasprowicz in the deep without further addition to the score.

Pietersen (23) and Flintoff (26) appeared to have weathered the storm and calmed the nerves with a vitally important fifth-wicket stand but Lee returned to account for both, the former caught behind and the Lancashire all-rounder bowled by a beauty. When Geraint Jones gifted Warne his 50th wicket of the year by holing out to Kasprowicz in the deep, it set up another tense and nervous finish with England still requiring 13.

However, when renowned blocker Hoggard hit a Lee full toss to the cover boundary the anticipation grew and Giles clipped Warne through midwicket for the 2 runs that won the match and provoked frenzied celebrations.

England captain Vaughan admitted his nerves had been shredded by the run chase but warned his team against complacency heading into the final Test.

'That kind of score is difficult to chase. If you are set 220 it is different – you just bat time. When you lose wickets trying to play your shots, the opposition gets momentum and it can be tricky, but I was delighted we got over the line,' he said.

'Once we got to within 4 to win we knew we were home, but up until that moment we knew they could have gone "bang, bang, bang" with the way Shane Warne and Brett Lee were bowling.

'Challenges have been thrown at us over the last few weeks, and we were asked whether we could sustain the performance in another challenge. We did that.

'We now realise we are on the brink of something special and the Oval will, I am sure, be an epic like the last three.'

Match-winner Giles revealed he was happier to be out in the thick of the action than watching from the balcony.

'It is a lot worse sitting up there than it was in the middle. Everyone is on edge, the dressing-room is very quiet and it is a "This can't be happening to us" sort of scenario,' he said.

Australia captain Ponting, meanwhile, said England's dominance early in the contest – when Man of the Match Flintoff's hundred and Jones' five-wicket haul forced Australia to follow on for the first time in 17 years was crucial.

'We just gave away too big a start. The first two days of the game is what cost us the Test match once again,' he said. 'The same goes for our batting, the wicket was very good and we didn't make as many as we should have done. We fought really hard but when you are that far behind you have to play exceptionally to win.

Fourth Test, Trent Bridge: Andrew Flintoff on his way to hammering a stunning 102 – his maiden Ashes century – to help England reach 477 all out at tea on the second day

Previous page: Aussie skipper Ricky Ponting is on the receiving end of England's aggressive attack, but he still manages to hit 156, the 23rd century of his Test career, as his team narrowly hold on for a draw

Marcus Trescothick spearheads England's bright start to the fourth Test with a half-century on the opening morning at Trent Bridge

Fourth Test, Trent Bridge: England swing bowler Matthew Hoggard celebrates trapping Australia's Matthew Hayden lbw for seven as he helps England extend their domination to the end of the second day. Hoggard takes three for 32 in an 11-over spell as Australia struggle to 99 for five at stumps

Controversy as Aussie skipper Ricky Ponting is run out (below, left) by England reserve Gary Pratt. He makes his displeasure at England's use of 12th men known during an exchange of words with Matthew Hoggard as he leaves the field (below) on day three at Trent Bridge

Andrew Strauss takes arguably the catch of the summer in the slips, diving horizontally at full-stretch to hang on to an edge from Adam Gilchrist off the bowling of Andrew Flintoff on the third day. England close in on what proves a nail-biting victory the next day, taking a 2-1 series lead going into the final Test match at The Oval

Fifth Test, The Oval: Shane Warne is not giving the Ashes up easily during what is probably the deadly Australian wrist-spinner's final Test match on English soil. He finishes the first day with five wickets, including this dismissal of Kevin Pietersen (left) with another of his leg-breaks

The brilliance of Shane Warne continues, setting up another nail-biting last day for England. But a breathtaking century from Kevin Pietersen (above) and another contribution from Ashley Giles, who celebrates a half-century (right) after earlier taking a great catch to end the Aussies' second innings, steers England home for a draw and a 2-1 series triumph

Michael Vaughan (facing page) savours the moment as his England side cling on for the draw that wins them the Ashes

Ashes heroes (from left) Andrew Flintoff with daughter Holly, Kevin Pietersen and Michael Vaughan celebrate on the team bus during the victory parade, which saw huge crowds line the streets of London (below)

'We had a little bit of a sniff thanks to some great bowling from Lee and Warne, but we just didn't have enough runs on the board.'

England win by three wickets
ENGLAND: second innings

M E Trescothick c Ponting b Warne 27
A J Strauss c Clarke b Warne 23
M P Vaughan c Hayden b Warne 0
I R Bell c Kasprowicz b Lee...3
K P Pietersen c Gilchrist b Lee 23
A Flintoff b Lee 26
G O Jones c Kasprowicz b Warne 3
A F Giles not out 7
M J Hoggard not out 8

Extras lb4 nb5 **9**
Total 7 wkts (31.5 overs) **129**

Fall: 1-32, 2-36, 3-57, 4-57, 5-103, 6-111, 7-116.
Did Not Bat: S J Harmison, S P Jones.
Bowling: Lee 12-0-51-3, **Kasprowicz** 2-0-19-0, **Warne** 13.5-2-31-4, **Tait** 4-0-24-0.

Man of the Match – Andrew Flintoff

Flintoff underlined his status as a national hero with his first Ashes century, thrashing Australia to all parts of Trent Bridge.

Typically, his innings was laced with numerous shots of sheer brute force. His attack completely altered the match situation, which had been delicately poised at 213 for four on his arrival at the crease.

Another wicket would have seriously damaged England's attempts to post an imposing first-innings total, but he batted sensibly late on the first day and then again when he lost partner Pietersen early the following morning.

But he found it impossible to hold back for too long and Flintoff in full flow is a prospect even the experienced Aussies do not relish.

His apparent disdain for bowlers, included those reckoned the world's best, is his greatest asset, but by the time he was out he had battered the initiative away from the tourists.

His innings, Flintoff's fifth Test century, obviously took a lot out of the big all-rounder as his bowling was not up to his usual standards in Australia's reply, and he went for nearly 5 an over. He was more than willing to share the second-innings bowling workload in the absence of Simon Jones, before chipping in with probably the best 26 he will ever make in a fraught run chase.

Flintoff at Trent Bridge

Batting: ....102 and 26
Bowling: ....11-1-54-1 and 29-4-83-2

Fifth Test Day One – Morning session

Warne struck three times in the morning session to prevent England racing to a commanding position in the deciding Ashes Test after they took an early advantage of batting-friendly conditions at the Oval.

Deciding to bat first after captain Michael Vaughan had won the toss – with four of the last six Tests on the ground won by the side batting first – England appeared to be on course for a commanding score.

But Warne, brought into the attack within the hour because of England's early onslaught, struck twice to leave them on a less promising total of 115 for three by the interval, with Strauss unbeaten on 42 and Pietersen on 10.

For the first time in the series England were forced to change their XI with Simon Jones failing to recover from an ankle injury. The vacant place went to Durham all-rounder Paul Collingwood, chosen primarily for his batting qualities.

Somerset left-hander Trescothick provided the early impetus with a number of boundaries giving England a flying start. He hit fast bowler Lee for two boundaries in one over, a feat repeated by Strauss four overs later. This forced Australia captain Ponting to remove his main spearhead from the attack after Lee conceded 21 runs in his first four overs.

Shaun Tait was little better and was also taken out of the attack after being hit for 15 in two overs and only McGrath, returning to the side after recovering from a right elbow injury, retained an element of control during the early onslaught.

But just 15 balls after coming into the attack as a replacement for Tait, Warne struck to end the productive 82-run opening stand when Trescothick pushed outside off stump and was brilliantly caught low down by Hayden at slip.

Trescothick had scored an aggressive 43, but Strauss picked up where he left off and continued England's momentum until Warne struck again six overs later to claim his second wicket for 10 runs in 15 balls.

Vaughan had looked comfortable in the batting-friendly conditions until he rocked onto the back foot in an attempt to force Warne onto the on side but instead picked out Clarke at midwicket to be caught for 11. England suffered a further blow when Bell was given lbw pushing forward to a slider.

ENGLAND: first innings

M E Trescothick c Hayden b Warne 43
A J Strauss not out 42
M P Vaughan c Clarke b Warne 11
I R Bell lbw b Warne 0
K P Pietersen not out 10

Extras b4 lb1 nb4 **9**
Total 3 wkts (27 overs) **115**

Fall: 1-82, 2-102, 3-104.
To Bat: A Flintoff, P D Collingwood, G O Jones, A F Giles,
M J Hoggard, S J Harmison.
Bowling: McGrath 11-2-29-0, **Lee** 4-1-21-0, **Tait** 5-0-33-0,
Warne 7-1-27-3.

Day One – Afternoon session

There was no let-up in the afternoon session as runs continued to come pretty easily, England adding a further 98 for the loss of just one wicket.

Strauss underlined the hosts' determination to end their long wait for Ashes success by contributing to a crucial fifth-wicket stand which guided England out of trouble. Needing only to avoid defeat to reclaim the Ashes, England were in a spot of bother at 131 for four after Warne picked up his fourth wicket of the day to continue his single-handed destruction of the top order.

Six overs after lunch he dismissed Hampshire colleague and close friend Pietersen, who played around a straight ball and was bowled off a pad for 14.

It took the determined joint effort of Strauss and Flintoff to guide England away from their perilous situation, and by tea they had progressed to a more promising 213 for four with an unbroken 82-run stand.

Strauss, a century-maker during the thrilling drawn Test at Old Trafford, was the mainstay of England's recovery and reached tea unbeaten on 92, which included 11 fours, having withstood Warne's superb spell either side of lunch.

The fall of Pietersen's wicket – Warne's 32nd of the series – gave the tourists a sniff of weakness, but Strauss and Flintoff, 39 not out, defied Australia's efforts for 21 overs until the interval and lifted England's hopes of reaching a first-innings total in excess of 450.

ENGLAND: first innings

(Continued: 115-3)

A J Strauss not out	92
M P Vaughan c Clarke b Warne	11
I R Bell lbw b Warne	0
K P Pietersen b Warne	14
A Flintoff not out	39

Extras b4 lb5 nb5 **14**
Total 4 wkts (55 overs) **213**

Fall: 1-82 2-102 3-104 4-131.
To Bat: P D Collingwood, G O Jones, A F Giles, M J Hoggard, S J Harmison.
Bowling: McGrath 15-2-44-0, **Lee** 10-1-44-0, **Tait** 9-0-47-0, **Warne** 18-3-55-4, **Katich** 3-0-14-0.

Day One – Evening session

Strauss scored his second century of the series but he was still overshadowed by Warne, who claimed his wicket in the final session to finish with five in the day as England were pegged back to 319 for seven.

The Middlesex left-hander required only 8 runs on the resumption after tea, and in Flintoff he had the ideal man with him to ease the pressure.

They had put on 82 in the afternoon session, and throughout their stand Strauss was happy to play a supporting role to Flintoff's powerful strokeplay.

Watched by wife Ruth in the crowd, and after more than four hours at the crease, Strauss brought up three figures with a four through midwicket off Lee.

He was immediately engulfed with a big Flintoff bear hug before accepting a standing ovation from another sell-out crowd.

Just as the crowd began to savour the possibility of Flintoff emulating Strauss' efforts, he attempted a late glance off McGrath and was caught low at slip by Warne for 72, which included a towering six off the leg-spinner and 12 fours. His stand with Strauss had been worth 143.

Flintoff's demise prompted an untimely loss of three wickets in nine overs. Collingwood, who had sat waiting with his pads on for more than two hours, fell six overs later, unluckily given leg before to Tait, while Warne returned to end Strauss' long defiance with a catch to Katich at silly point.

Strauss, who hit 17 boundaries during his superb 129, provided Warne with his fifth wicket and left him needing only three more victims to have claimed the most England Test wickets in history, eclipsing Dennis Lillee's total of 167.

Geraint Jones (21 not out) and Ashley Giles (5 not out) added a further 22 before the close.

Strauss felt his seventh Test hundred was the best of the lot but claimed he did not enjoy a minute of it as England began the Ashes decider tentatively.

'In terms of importance it is the best I have ever played. It was a massive day in the context of the series and it was vital that one of us went on and got a hundred,' said the England opener.

'I didn't really enjoy it at any stage because of the game situation; there was not a time at which we didn't feel under pressure.

'The high level of expectation has been very hard to get away from over the last week or so. That is what has made this game so exciting to be part of.'

'He had a bit of luck, but you have to give him credit, it doesn't matter how you look when you get there. A hundred is a hundred,' reflected Warne, who claimed Strauss' wicket for the fifth time in nine innings.

'We were staring down the barrel. It has been a trademark of the series that England get ahead and we fight back,' he added after bowling 34 overs in the day.

'The momentum out there was swinging all the time throughout the day, but we have just got our noses in front.

'Hopefully some of the guys with the new ball can get those wickets pretty quickly in the morning so I can get my feet up because I am tired.'

ENGLAND: first innings

(Continued: 213-4)

A J Strauss c Katich b Warne	129
M P Vaughan c Clarke b Warne	11
I R Bell lbw b Warne	0
K P Pietersen b Warne	14
A Flintoff c Warne b McGrath	72
P D Collingwood bw b Tait	7
G O Jones not out	21
A F Giles not out	5

Extras b4 lb6 nb7 **17**

Total 7 wkts (88 overs) **319**

Fall: 1-82 2-102 3-104 4-131 5-274 6-289 7-297.
To Bat: M J Hoggard, S J Harmison.
Bowling: McGrath 19-5-48-1, **Lee** 17-3-68-0, **Tait** 15-1-61-1, **Warne** 34-4-118-5, **Katich** 3-0-14-0.

Shrugging off Warne's taunts, England's Andrew Strauss was the only player to score two tons in the series.

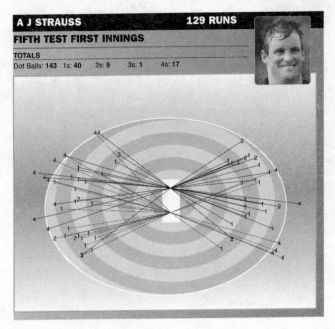

A J STRAUSS   **129 RUNS**

FIFTH TEST FIRST INNINGS

TOTALS
Dot Balls: **143**   1s: **40**   2s: **9**   3s: **1**   4s: **17**

Day Two – Morning session

England's tailenders contributed crucial runs to thwart Australia's hopes of wrapping up their innings quickly and claiming an important advantage on the second morning.

Resuming on a disappointing 319 for seven, England were hoping wicketkeeper Geraint Jones, who hit 85 to help win the fourth Test at Trent Bridge, could guide them towards a competitive first-innings total of around 400.

But instead of Jones propelling England forward, it was the tailenders who again contributed useful runs to help them reach 373 after defying Australia's efforts to wrap up the innings quickly.

Jones, 21 not out overnight, started brightly by cutting fast bowler Lee for the first boundary of the day in the second over.

Lee responded superbly to that early blow by knocking back Jones' off stump with the next ball, a full-length delivery which evaded a defensive forward lunge and earned Australia an early breakthrough. But it was a further 11 overs before the tourists tasted success again with Giles and Hoggard – the heroes of Trent Bridge where they guided England to tense triumph – combining again in a determined 20-run stand.

Hoggard was perhaps fortunate to survive a dropped slip chance before he had scored when he edged McGrath and Langer was unable to take the catch, diving across Warne from second slip.

Giles could also count himself as lucky later in the same over when he appeared to edge behind, confirmed by television replays – only for umpire Rudi Koertzen to deny Australia's claims.

Koertzen's rejection of their appeal annoyed Australia captain Ponting, who continued his protests at the end of the over, but only had to wait two further overs before McGrath finally ended the stubborn stand.

Hoggard had batted for 46 minutes for his two runs when he was finally outwitted by McGrath's slower ball, which he chipped straight to Martyn at wide mid-off, but England's resistance was still not broken.

Instead of crumbling, Harmison went on the offensive, contributing a useful 20 to a 28-run last-wicket stand off only 31 balls that took England past 350.

The partnership was finally ended when Warne, introduced into the attack in a desperate attempt to wrap up the innings, won an lbw appeal against Giles despite him pushing well forward to claim his 34th wicket of the series and match his best Ashes tally set in 1993.

Facing a tricky seven overs before lunch, Australia's openers Langer and Hayden survived the new ball spells from Harmison and Hoggard to reach 19 without loss at the interval.

ENGLAND: first innings

(Continued: 319-7)

G O Jones b Lee	25
A F Giles lbw b Warne	32
M J Hoggard c Martyn b McGrath	2
S J Harmison not out	20

Extras b4 lb6 w1 nb7 **18**
Total (105.3 overs) **373**

Fall: 1-82, 2-102, 3-104, 4-131, 5-274, 6-289, 7-297, 8-325, 9-345.

Bowling: McGrath 27-5-72-2, **Lee** 23-3-94-1, **Tait** 15-1-61-1, **Warne** 37.3-5-122-6, **Katich** 3-0-14-0.

AUSTRALIA: first innings

J L Langer not out	16
M L Hayden not out	2

Extras nb11
Total 0 wkts (7 overs) **19**

To Bat: R T Ponting, D R Martyn, M J Clarke, S M Katich, A C Gilchrist, S K Warne, S W Tait, G D McGrath.

Bowling: Harmison 4-1-8-0, **Hoggard** 3-0-11-0.

Day Two – Afternoon session

England's hopes of mounting a fightback in the afternoon session were frustrated by Australia's best opening partnership of the summer at the Oval.

Resuming on 19 for no wicket, Australia's misfiring batting line-up finally found some consistent form.

Openers Langer and Hayden forged a century stand and guided Australia to a convincing 112 without loss at tea after exposing the limitations of England's gamble to include only four specialist bowlers in their line-up.

Langer was the more aggressive of the pair, as Hayden was still searching for the fluency which had escaped him during the series, and claimed his third half-century of the summer off only 63 balls.

He reached that landmark by hitting 14 off the opening over from left-arm spinner Giles, which included two sixes in three balls, and set the tempo for the tourists while Hayden concentrated on giving his partner as much of the strike as possible.

England's only chance of making the breakthrough came through all-rounder Collingwood, preferred to James Anderson as replacement for the injured Simon Jones, who almost ended Langer's threatening innings with his eighth delivery.

Attempting to cut a ball which was too close to his body, Langer edged to Trescothick at slip but he dropped the chance after diving high to his right and enabled Australia's opener to escape on 53.

While Langer raced to an unbeaten 75 at tea, Hayden struggled and took 81 minutes to reach double figures when he cut Harmison for only his second boundary, but by tea had progressed to 32.

AUSTRALIA: first innings
(Continued: 19-0)

J L Langer not out **75**
M L Hayden not out **32**
                                        Extras lb2 nb3 **5**
                        Total 0 wkts (33 overs) **112**
To Bat: R T Ponting, D R Martyn, M J Clarke, S M Katich, A C Gilchrist, S K Warne, S W Tait, G D McGrath.
Bowling: Harmison 8-1-21-0, **Hoggard** 7-1-21-0, **Flintoff** 7-2-20-0, **Giles** 7-0-31-0, **Collingwood** 4-0-17-0.

Day Two – Evening session

Australia's gamble with the London weather provided England with encouragement that they could still complete an historic Ashes success despite struggling to remain competitive in the deciding Test.

The visitors were progressing nicely with their first century opening partnership of the series to reach 112 without loss as they prepared for a 37-over final session.

But instead of forcing home their advantage in the time remaining, Australia instead adopted a cautious approach and accepted an offer of bad light from umpires Billy Bowden and Koertzen before a ball could be bowled after tea.

Facing a tricky dilemma of whether to bat on to reduce England's 261-run lead, risking the loss of several quick wickets, or to take the light, Langer (75 not out) and Hayden (32) opted for safety-first cricket.

With possible light showers forecast for Saturday set to further disrupt Australia's continuity it was a decision that could backfire on the tourists if they ran out of time to force home their advantage.

Langer defended the decision, which captain Ponting and deputy Gilchrist plumped for during a tea-time discussion but which surprised England's players as well as watching supporters and commentators.

'I asked Ricky and Gilly what their thoughts were and they thought it was the same as any other Test match,' he said.

'When we walked out, anyone could see it was very dark, Flintoff was reverse swinging the ball and we felt it was best to play him in the best conditions possible. Of course we thought we could get back on.

'We would have loved to have kept batting, but when we weighed up the options, if we had lost a wicket, the new batsman would have had to face the reverse-swinging ball in dark conditions.

'Unfortunately we have no control over rain or light, only one person in the world does and he is not sat in our room. All we have lost is half an hour or an hour of play and the way the series has gone most games have been settled in four days.'

'We were a little bit surprised with the decision, but you can understand it because if we had got two or three quick wickets they would have been on the back foot,' said a sympathetic Giles.

'I don't think they would have been too scared of facing me in bad light. But Freddie bowling at 90 miles per hour-plus when it is dark is a bit of a handful.

'Of course I hope they live to regret it but there are three days left and that is a lot of time.

'Ricky Ponting cannot, and we cannot, afford to cloud-watch: it is important we stay focused on the game rather than watching out for weather forecasts. If your mind is off the game the side we are playing against can be dangerous.'

Day Three – Morning session

Hayden claimed his first half-century of the series during the weather-hit third morning as England struggled to make a breakthrough.

Hayden reached the landmark in determined fashion as Australia's hopes of building on their promising start were disrupted by rain both before the start and during the session.

Resuming 261 runs adrift on 112 without loss following their controversial decision to accept the offer to go off for bad light, Australia had hoped to build on their good start.

But instead, the weather again intervened, firstly to delay the start for half an hour and then to interrupt for a further 30 minutes, which restricted Australia to 157 without loss, adding only 45 runs in the 14 overs available.

England were also conscious of the need to restrict Australia's advance towards a major first-innings lead and strove for an early breakthrough.

Yorkshire seamer Hoggard believed he had secured a wicket with the first ball of the day when he appealed for lbw against Langer, but his claims were rejected by umpire Bowden.

Langer almost gifted England their first wicket in Hoggard's next over, calling a quick single and setting off without seeing Collingwood rushing in from cover to almost throw down the stumps before Hayden could reach the other end.

Hayden, who had resumed on 32 aiming to score his first half-century of the series, was also fortunate later that over with an uppish cover drive that sped past Collingwood's dive to the boundary.

Needing a big score to safeguard his place in Australia's line-up after scoring only 180 runs previously in the series, Hayden could also count himself lucky another risky drive off Hoggard flew wide of Strauss' dive at third slip. That shot took him to within 4 of his 50.

He had moved within 3 of that landmark when rain stopped play in mid-morning, but it only kept players off the field for half an hour and he quickly claimed the 3 runs required for his half-century – which he marked in understated fashion and barely acknowledged the applause around the Oval.

By lunch Hayden was on 60 while Langer, who scored only 26 runs during the session, was also in sight of his first century of the series.

AUSTRALIA: first innings
(Overnight: 112-0)

```
J L Langer not out ......................................................................91
M L Hayden not out ....................................................................60
                                                   Extras  lb2 nb4 6
                                        Total 0 wkts (47 overs) 157
```
To Bat: R T Ponting, D R Martyn, M J Clarke, S M Katich, A C Gilchrist, S K Warne, S W Tait, G D McGrath.
Bowling: Harmison 10-1-29-0, Hoggard 14-1-53-0, Flintoff 12-5-25-0, Giles 7-0-31-0, Collingwood 4-0-17-0.

Day Three – Afternoon session

England's hopes of completing an historic Ashes success were lifted by the weather when Australia's march towards a crucial lead was hampered by further regular showers.

Fewer than six overs were possible between lunch and tea as Australia added 28 to progress to 185 for one with Langer completing his first century of the series.

Hayden, meanwhile, was unbeaten on 70 with his sights set on breaking a 17-Test run without reaching three figures.

The regular interruptions only served to underline the major gamble Australia had made the evening before, with Langer and Hayden choosing once again to accept an offer of bad light.

In the play that was possible there was time enough for both Langer to reach his century and Harmison to claim England's first breakthrough during a hostile over from the Pavilion End.

The Durham paceman's over included a cut for four by Langer to bring up his century (which contained two sixes and 11 fours) and an uppercut for another boundary to reach 104 and become the eighth Australian batsman to reach 7,000 Test runs.

The over also included two wides from deliveries that flew over Langer's head, and Harmison was also no-balled for attempting a third bouncer before striking to claim an overdue success for England.

Langer had battled for nearly four hours for his century, but got an inside edge on to his stumps via a thigh off the back foot and walked off furious with himself.

And his frustration was heightened by rain calling a halt to any further play before new batsman Ponting could even get down the pavilion steps.

AUSTRALIA: first innings
(Continued: 157-0)

J L Langer b Harmison **105**
M L Hayden not out...**70**
Extras lb3 w2 nb5 **10**
Total 1 wkt (52.4 overs) **185**

Fall: 1-185.
To Bat: R T Ponting, D R Martyn, M J Clarke, S M Katich,
A C Gilchrist, S K Warne, S W Tait, G D McGrath.
Bowling: Harmison 12.4-1-43-1, **Hoggard** 14-1-53-0, **Flintoff** 12-5-25-0, **Giles** 10-0-44-0, **Collingwood** 4-0-17-0.

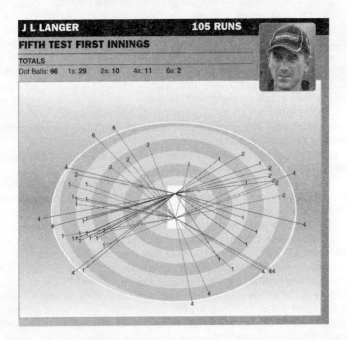

Day Three – Evening session

Flintoff added another notable feat to his staggering list of achievements this summer, but still ended up playing a supporting role to the weather.

The Lancashire all-rounder became only the second man in history to score 300 runs and take 20 wickets in a series against Australia, emulating Ian Botham in the legendary 1981 series. But for all Flintoff's efforts, it was the south London weather which exerted the greatest influence on the outcome of the match after restricting Australia's advance towards a potentially decisive first-innings lead.

After a shortened afternoon session the tourists put on 92 after tea for the loss of one wicket with the highlight for them being Hayden's century as they advanced to 277 for two by the time bad light ended play 5.1 overs prematurely.

But with only two possible days remaining time appeared to be running out for them to secure the victory they required to retain the Ashes. Hayden ended a 17-Test barren run without a century by resisting his natural attacking game and instead building a century during an occupation of the crease lasting nearly five hours. He was given solid support by captain Ponting, who was fortunate to be given a reprieve on 13 when he was caught at silly point by Bell off Giles – only for umpire Bowden to once again reject England's claims. Fortunately for England, that decision was not that costly as Flintoff returned for one last spell and claimed the breakthrough with his second ball, getting one to lift and enticing Ponting into edging to Strauss at gully for 35.

Martyn should have followed in Flintoff's next over, when he attempted an uppercut which immediately prompted an appeal from the big Lancastrian – but the appeal was rejected by umpire Koertzen, perhaps because none of England's slips joined in.

Television replays later suggested Flintoff was right to appeal and just three overs later bad light ended another frustrating day.

Flintoff, ever the fighter, urged his team-mates to give every last ounce of effort in their bid to seal Ashes success even though Australia were now just 96 runs behind.

'The Australians have got their noses in front, but we have scrapped and fought for a long time now and we have put in some special performances,' he said. 'We have two days left and we have to give it everything. Every ounce of energy we have got in our tanks has to be left out there on the pitch.

'We have shown on many occasions the character, will and strength of this side and that will have to be called upon again – and we are confident we can do that. There is so much at stake at this stage that there are not too many people complaining of being tired.'

Hayden, who finished unbeaten on 110, entered the match playing for his international future and responded with an innings of rare

The strain of carrying England's attack shows as Freddie can barely muster the energy for the obligatory 'high-fives'.

resilience which even got the approval of Flintoff, who marked the left-handed opener's landmark with a pat on the back. 'The series as a whole has been played in a great spirit,' added Flintoff.

'It is the two best sides in the world going head-to-head, and it has been a great advert for cricket.

'It has been competitive, the odd word has been said here and there in the middle but afterwards we have got on well, we have been in each other's dressing-rooms, having a beer and talking things over.'

AUSTRALIA: first innings

(Continued: 185-1)

J L Langer b Harmison	105
M L Hayden not out	110
R T Ponting c Strauss b Flintoff	35
D R Martyn not out	9

Extras b4 lb6 w2 nb6 **18**
Total 2 wkts (78.4 overs) **277**

Fall: 1-185 2-264
To Bat: M J Clarke, S M Katich, A C Gilchrist, S K Warne, S W Tait, G D McGrath.
Bowling: Harmison 20-2-75-1, **Hoggard** 14-1-53-0, **Flintoff** 19.4-7-48-1, **Giles** 21- 0-74-0, **Collingwood** 4-0-17-0.

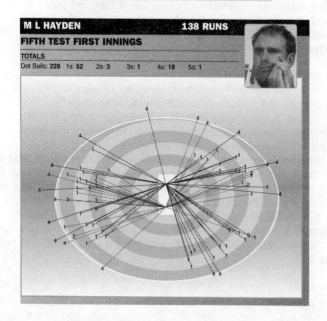

M L HAYDEN   **138 RUNS**

FIFTH TEST FIRST INNINGS

TOTALS

Dot Balls: **228**   1s: **52**   2s: **3**   3s: **1**   4s: **18**   5s: **1**

Day Four – Morning session

Flintoff delivered another stirring display of hostile bowling as England desperately fought to prevent Australia gaining a major lead.

The Lancashire all-rounder spearheaded England's fightback on the fourth morning with a marathon 11.2-over spell unchanged from the Pavilion End.

And he lifted England's hopes of halting Australia's push for victory by claiming three for 13 in 46 balls as the tourists slipped from 277 for two to 356 for six at lunch, still trailing by 17 runs.

The tourists knew they would have to battle through bad light if they were to have any chance of building up a big enough lead for Warne to exert his influence on the final day.

But losing regular wickets did not feature as part of their strategy – with Flintoff regularly checking their momentum during his superb spell, starting by claiming Martyn's scalp in the second over of the day.

Martyn, who had scored only one half-century during the series, added just 1 run to his overnight 9 before he was surprised by the extra bounce and could only loop his attempted pull straight to Collingwood. Having claimed the early breakthrough, captain Vaughan took the new ball to test Australia's resolve in less than perfect light, which also conversely affected England's efforts in the field.

England almost claimed a second wicket just four overs after claiming the new ball with Matthew Hoggard inducing an edge from Clarke which Flintoff was unable to hold at second slip.

He made amends for that error by finally ending Hayden's near seven-hour innings when he claimed the first of two lbws which effectively halted Australia's progress.

Hayden had hit 18 boundaries in his determined 138, but was undone by a full-length delivery striking his pads. Umpire Koertzen had no hesitation in raising his finger, with Hayden only half-forward down the pitch.

Katich followed in Flintoff's next over in identical fashion and Hoggard got his reward for a lively new ball spell by claiming the important scalp of Gilchrist, also trapped lbw, in the final over before lunch.

AUSTRALIA: first innings
(Overnight: 277-2)

M L Hayden lbw b Flintoff **138**
D R Martyn c Collingwood b Flintoff **10**
M J Clarke not out **23**
S M Katich lbw b Flintoff **1**
A C Gilchrist lbw b Hoggard **23**
                                                        Extras b4 lb7 w2 nb8 **21**
                                              Total 6 wkts (101.1 overs) **356**
Fall: 1-185, 2-264, 3-281, 4-323, 5-329, 6-356.
To Bat: S K Warne, S W Tait, G D McGrath.
Bowling: Harmison 22-2-87-1, **Hoggard** 21.1-1-93-1, **Flintoff** 31-10-72-4, **Giles** 23-3-1-76-0, **Collingwood** 4-0-17-0.

Day Four – Afternoon session

South London's weather conditions lifted England's hopes of claiming the Ashes after Flintoff completed his five-wicket haul to dismiss Australia.

The Lancashire all-rounder finished with five for 78 runs, only the second five-wicket haul of his Test career, after accounting for leg-spinner Warne.

It helped to bowl out the tourists for 367 and earn a 6-run lead. But once again it was the weather which provided the biggest help with bad light halting play after England had slumped to 7 for one by mid-afternoon.

Flintoff struck after lunch when Warne mistimed an attempted pull which Vaughan claimed at mid-on at the second attempt.

But it was Hoggard who provided the finishing touches to England's revival, earning a shock first-innings lead.

He removed Lee and McGrath – his first dismissal of the series – in quick succession in a spell either side of lunch which brought four wickets for as many runs in 19 balls.

With the bad light persisting, Australia introduced Warne into the attack in only the fourth over after the umpires warned them they would offer the light to England's batsmen should Australia persist with the seamers. It was a tactic which brought immediate rewards with Strauss edging his fourth ball to Katich at short leg via a pad.

But Australia were unable to build on that breakthrough with England accepting a further offer to go off for bad light just one over later and an early tea was taken at 2.30 p.m. with the score at 7 for one.

It was a controversial move with Australia ready to employ

spinners at both ends, but umpire Koerzten said they were trying to be consistent.

'With the fast bowlers there is an acceptable level and, as soon as it dips below that level, you offer the light to the batsmen,' he insisted.

'In this case, with spin bowlers on, we give them a bit more leeway but, once we think it's unfair, that's when we offer the light and we won't go back on until the reading improves.'

AUSTRALIA: first innings

(Continued: 356-6)

R T Ponting c Strauss b Flintoff	35
D R Martyn c Collingwood b Flintoff	10
M J Clarke lbw b Hoggard	25
S M Katich lbw b Flintoff	1
A C Gilchrist lbw b Hoggard	23
S K Warne c Vaughan b Flintoff	0
B Lee c Giles b Hoggard	6
G D McGrath c Strauss b Hoggard	0
S W Tait not out	1

Extras b4 lb8 w2 nb9 **23**
Total (107.1 overs) **367**
Fall: 1-185, 2-264, 3-281, 4-323, 5-329, 6-356, 7-359, 8-363, 9-363.
Bowling: Harmison 22-2-87-1, **Hoggard** 24.1-2-97-4, **Flintoff** 34-10-78-5, **Giles** 23-1-76-0, **Collingwood** 4-0-17-0.

Day Four – Evening session

The bad light which brought the players off for an early tea returned in the final session to frustrate Australia, in particular Warne.

A minor improvement in conditions convinced the officials a resumption of play was possible, and the teams took the field again at 3.10 p.m.

However, they were out there for only half an hour before the batsmen were offered the light once again at 34 for one despite Warne bowling in tandem with left-arm spinner Clarke.

Ironically, Vaughan twice cut fast bowler McGrath for four prior to the officials requiring slow bowlers to operate from both ends if play were to continue.

Warne stayed out in the middle for several minutes contesting the umpires' decision after England had progressed to 34 for one, a lead of just 40, with a further 53 overs of the day remaining.

His protests were in vain though and with the light failing to improve no further play was possible. Vaughan finished the day on 19 not out, with opening batsman Trescothick unbeaten on 14. But there was no doubt about the star of the day, with Hoggard hailing fellow bowler Flintoff for his crucial five-wicket haul earlier in the day.

'He bowled a magnificent spell. The team-talk was that we only had one bowling day left and that might mean 98 overs, but thankfully Freddie [Flintoff] put in a Herculean effort and we managed to bowl them out,' he said.

'I don't think we could have asked for a better day when we arrived at the ground in the morning.

'We put the ball in the right areas, Australia had to force the pace to get runs on the board and thankfully we bowled them out before they got a lead.'

Australia coach John Buchanan also had praise for the Lancashire all-rounder, insisting it was he rather than poor visibility which hastened Australia's demise.

'We were keen to maintain the way we were batting. If the light had got so bad that our batsmen felt it was time to leave the crease they'd have done that,' he said.

'But they felt pretty comfortable out there right from the word go. It wasn't necessarily a case of bad light that saw our wickets fall; great credit to Flintoff who took the ball from one end and pounded in.'

The early finish brought the Ashes urn ever nearer, but Hoggard admitted there was plenty of work to be done before anyone could start celebrating.

'It now turns into a one-innings match and they could be chasing a target off 20 overs. It could be another fantastic Test,' said the Yorkshire seamer.

'It would be nice to go through the day without losing wickets, but this series has always had a twist in the tail.

'We know we will have to bat well, it is by no means over – we are playing the best team in the world and we have Warne to contend with.'

The prospect of an historic triumph even got the 23,000 crowd – who paid an average of £50 per ticket – greeting the sight of the players leaving the middle with huge cheers.

'It makes a change from being jeered for coming off for a few spots of rain,' admitted Hoggard.

'To bring home the Ashes will be fantastic, not just for us but for every sport in this country. Even David Beckham has been talking about it: football talking about cricket has never happened, it is just massive for cricket to get into the headlines.'

ENGLAND: second innings

M E Trescothick not out...**14**
A J Strauss c Katich b Warne **1**
M P Vaughan not out **19**
Total 1 wkt (13.2 overs) **34**

Fall: 1-2.
To Bat: I R Bell, K P Pietersen, A Flintoff, P D Collingwood,
G O Jones, A F Giles, M J Hoggard, S J Harmison.
Bowling: McGrath 5-0-13-0, **Lee** 1-1-0-0, **Warne** 5.2-0-15-1,
Clarke 2-0-6-0.

Day Five – Morning session

The irrepressible Warne claimed another record in his remarkable
career as England's hopes of winning the Ashes suffered a huge blow
on the final morning at the Oval.

He struck twice in the session to claim his 168th English victim,
breaking Dennis Lillee's record of the most Test wickets against
England and setting up another nerve-wracking finale.

His efforts were matched by McGrath, who claimed two wickets
off successive balls as England slumped to 127 for five at lunch, a lead
of just 133.

It was not the morning England fans had gathered in their droves
to witness. The ground was packed to the rafters and spectators
without tickets were perched on rooftops, hanging out of windows
and clinging to every possible vantage point with high expectations
as England resumed 40 runs ahead on 34 for one.

The hosts' best hope of securing the Ashes was to resist
Australia's efforts to dismiss them cheaply in order to chase a
victory target on the final afternoon.

They succeeded in that objective for the first nine overs with
captain Vaughan, who had resumed overnight on 19, hitting a flurry
of early boundaries to lift England's confidence during the early
stages.

But just as England's fans in the capacity Oval crowd began to
relax, however, Australia struck twice in as many balls to once again
put a nation on the edge of its seat and leave the outcome of the series
in the balance.

Vaughan had progressed to 45 when he pushed forward
defensively but edged McGrath behind. Wicketkeeper Gilchrist took
a brilliant diving catch to his right to claim the first breakthrough.

The captain's demise brought Bell to the crease aiming to bounce
back from his first-innings duck but instead suffered a pair when he
edged the very next ball straight to Warne at first slip.

Warne can feel the Ashes slipping away. Collingwood is in the background.

McGrath thought he had claimed a hat-trick with the next delivery when a short ball flicked Pietersen's shoulder and was caught behind. But the Hampshire batsman survived the lengthy appeals with umpire Bowden remaining unmoved.

It was the first of a number of close shaves for Pietersen as he desperately attempted to rebuild England's innings, including almost running himself out after progressing to 9 when he pushed to mid-on, took a quick single and only just reached the non-striker's end before Clarke threw down the stumps.

Pietersen was given another major reprieve in the next over when Lee was introduced as McGrath's replacement and almost struck with his fourth ball, a full-length delivery edged straight to Warne at first slip which this time he put down. His reaction to that escape was to go on the attack against Warne in the next over, launching him for two sixes over midwicket, which gave England confidence they had overcome the worst. But Warne struck again in his next over to trap Trescothick leg before with a fiercely turning leg-break, which pinned him in front of his stumps and took Lillee's proud record.

He claimed his 37th victim of this series just four overs later, removing England's main threat by taking a smart return catch off all-rounder Flintoff.

ENGLAND: second innings
(Continued: 34-1)

M E Trescothick lbw b Warne	33
M P Vaughan c Gilchrist b McGrath	45
i R Bell c Warne b McGrath	0
K P Pietersen not out	35
A Flintoff c & b Warne	8
P D Collingwood not out	0
	Extras w5 **5**
	Total 5 wkts (39 overs) **127**

Fall: 1-2, 2-67, 3-67, 4-109, 5-126.
To Bat: G O Jones, A F Giles, M J Hoggard, S J Harmison.
Bowling: McGrath 13-2-37-2, **Lee** 8-1-29-0, **Warne** 16-0-55-3, **Clarke** 2-0-6-0.

Day Five – Afternoon session

A thrilling series swung back in England's favour during an enthralling two hours in which Pietersen single-handedly turned things around with his maiden Test century in only his fifth match.

The Hampshire batsman did enjoy a huge slice of luck on his way to three figures, being dropped three times, but his timely innings

Tait's veins bulge as he gives Geraint Jones the send-off.

helped steer England to a more comfortable 221 for seven at tea, leading by 227 with a maximum of 49 overs remaining.

Australia came out for the afternoon session scenting victory after claiming four wickets before lunch but they found Pietersen, who moved to his 50 in 70 balls having hit three sixes and two fours, in determined mood.

He was ably supported by Durham all-rounder Collingwood, who helped construct a 60-run stand for the sixth wicket at almost a run a ball.

Pietersen's aggressive approach does provide opportunities for the fielding side, and one arrived just four overs after lunch when the South African-born batsman pulled Lee down to the fine-leg boundary where the diving Tait could not hold on to a difficult chance.

Pietersen was on 60 at the time and the drop was to prove costly for the tourists. He then set about Lee, hammering him for 37 off his first three overs after lunch to dominate the partnership with Collingwood.

The stand was only broken, with the total having raced on to 186, when Collingwood pushed forward to Warne and was caught at silly point by Ponting.

Tait managed to make a contribution shortly before tea by removing Geraint Jones' off stump when the wicketkeeper had made only 1, but Pietersen's mixture of solid defence and outrageous strokeplay guided England to tea and in sight of the draw which would begin an Oval Ashes party. He brought up his century with a driven four through the covers, sparking a huge outpouring of emotion from him, his team-mates on the dressing-room balcony and the entire ground.

Pietersen reached the interval unbeaten on 105, which included four sixes and 10 fours. Ashley Giles kept him company with 6 not out.

ENGLAND: second innings

(Continued: 127-5)

K P Pietersen not out	105
A Flintoff c & b Warne	8
P D Collingwood c Ponting b Warne	10
G O Jones b Tait	1
A F Giles not out	6

Extras b4 w6 nb2 **12**

Total 7 wkts (63 overs) **221**

Fall: 1-2, 2-67, 3-67, 4-109, 5-126, 6-186, 7-199.

To Bat: M J Hoggard, S J Harmison.

Bowling: McGrath 18-3-44-2, **Lee** 11-1-66-0, **Warne** 28-2-74-4, **Clarke** 2-0-6-0, **Tait** 4-0-27-1.

Day Five – Evening session

The man to snatch victory from Australia's grasp and smash it into a thousand pieces was Pietersen, who compiled a knock of 158 so devastating and so thrilling that you could only marvel at his achievement.

Having ridden his luck to reach 105 not out at tea early dismissal would have given the Aussies the slightest glimmer of hope they could possibly make a dart at a target of about 250 in a frantic run chase.

That did not materialise as Pietersen, who had now warmed to the occasion, continued his assault on the much-vaunted bowling attack.

When he was eventually out to a classic McGrath leg-cutter which struck the top of off stump in the third over with the new ball the Oval rose as a man to salute an outstanding innings.

In it he had smashed seven sixes and 15 fours. That set a new record for the number of sixes hit in one Ashes Test match, eclipsing the six Ian Botham had registered in the 1981 series. It also left Pietersen as the highest run-scorer in the series.

His knock had single-handedly saved the Test and secured the Ashes as the lead had been extended to 308 in an eighth-wicket stand of 109 with Giles and that was way beyond Australia's means.

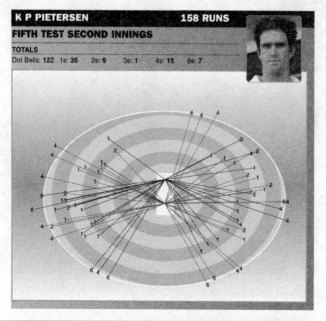

K P PIETERSEN   158 RUNS
FIFTH TEST SECOND INNINGS
TOTALS
Dot Balls: 122   1s: 35   2s: 9   3s: 1   4s: 15   6s: 7

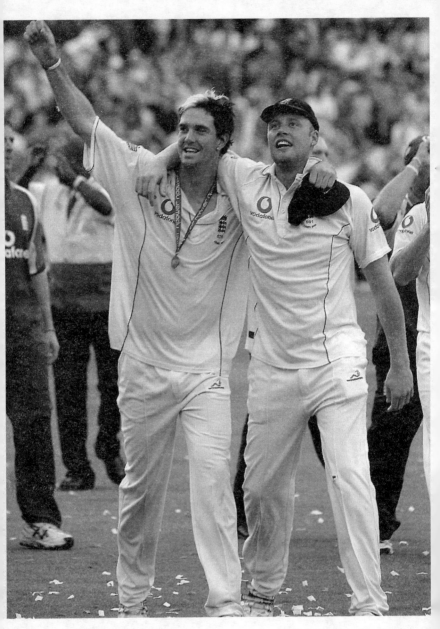

England heroes Pietersen and Flintoff.

Warne congratulates his friend and rival Pietersen.

Pietersen's was the second standing ovation of the day, the first coming at the conclusion of Warne's marathon spell of 31 overs from the Vauxhall End.

Warne, due to celebrate his 36th birthday the next day, was playing his final Test in this country, having become the most successful bowler against England in history. Even Pietersen's departure did not end the punishment for Australia as Giles went on to complete his half-century.

He was eventually dismissed by Warne for 59 and Harmison followed two balls later as the legendary leg-spinner finished with six for 124 and 40 wickets for the series. That return was largely immaterial though, as the Ashes had effectively gone.

England were greeted vociferously when they took to the field to send down the three overs required for the contest to be agreed a stalemate.

However, Harmison sent down only four deliveries before Australia accepted the offer of bad light and the inevitable was put on hold.

In anti-climactic circumstances at 6.15 p.m. the nation was granted the end result it craved when umpires Bowden and Koertzen returned to the middle to remove the bails, and the celebrations began to commemorate a first series win in nine attempts against the world's No.1 side.

History had been made.

Match drawn
ENGLAND: second innings

(Continued: 221-7)

K P Pietersen b McGrath	158
A Flintoff c & b Warne	8
P D Collingwood c Ponting b Warne	10
G O Jones b Tait	1
A F Giles b Warne	59
M J Hoggard not out	4
S J Harmison c Hayden b Warne	0

Extras b4 w7 nb5 **16**
Total (91.3 overs) **335**

Fall: 1-2, 2-67, 3-67, 4-109, 5-126, 6-186, 7-199, 8-308, 9-335.
Bowling: McGrath 26-3-85-3, **Lee** 20-4-88-0, **Warne** 38.3-3-124-6, **Clarke** 2-0-6-0, **Tait** 5-0 -28-1.

AUSTRALIA: second innings

J L Langer not out	0
M L Hayden not out	0

Extras lb4 **4**
Total 0 wkts (0.4 overs) **4**

Did Not Bat: R T Ponting, D R Martyn, M J Clarke, S M Katich, A C Gilchrist, S K Warne, S W Tait, G D McGrath.
Bowling: Harmison 0.4-0-0-0.

Man of the match – Kevin Pietersen

Pietersen announced his arrival on the Test match scene with three consecutive half-centuries.

But the South African-born batsman really became a Test match player with a savage knock that not only saved the crucial final match, but secured the Ashes for England.

It is one thing to blaze away in the opening exchanges of a series, it is another to produce such an exhilarating innings when you have a nation hanging expectantly on every single delivery and Warne, on top of his game, sensing weakness. Flintoff's displays, suddenly making the front page of the tabloids, had put Pietersen in the shade in the middle part of the series.

But the Hampshire batsman, with his blonde streak and diamond earrings, is not a man to be happy in the shadows.

He will have believed it was his destiny to play the innings of his life with the whole world watching but even the super-confident Pietersen must have wondered what was in store as he strode to the crease with England wobbling at 67 for three looking to bat out the day and salvage a draw.

Not even in his wildest dreams could he have imagined he would be able to transfer his devastating one-day international form into the Test arena.

The ploy to be positive could have backfired spectacularly, and it would have cost England the match and ultimately the Ashes. But the fact Pietersen backed himself was all that mattered and when he eventually departed to a rousing standing ovation he had repaid in full the faith shown in him.

Pietersen at the Oval
Batting: ....14 and 158

Players of the series

Andrew Flintoff

The Lancashire all-rounder turned in some truly memorable performances with both bat and ball in the series, and proved just how pivotal he is to England in the No.6 position.

What was equally – if not more – important was the timing of his interventions, especially his knack of taking wickets at crucial times.

When England appeared to be looking for inspiration in the field, captain Michael Vaughan invariably threw the ball to Flintoff, and his whole-hearted approach often brought the breakthrough required.

His ability to reverse-swing the ball, shared by Simon Jones, was a major factor in preventing Australia making a score over 400 throughout the entire five Tests.

Only a select few bowlers can effectively utilise the art of reverse swing, and Australia certainly found it difficult to play Flintoff as he consistently bowled at more than 90 mph in the middle of an innings.

Probably his most telling contribution with the ball came in the final Test at the Oval, when his five-wicket haul pegged back Australia just as they were looking to push on past England's total.

It would be no exaggeration to say that his wickets were crucial to England's success in playing out five days for a draw, which was enough to reclaim the famous urn.

Flintoff's batting, of course, has always been his stand-out quality and his first Ashes century was a just reward, although his 73 in the 180 all out in the second innings at Edgbaston did just as much to win the match as the 177-run sixth-wicket stand with Geraint Jones at Trent Bridge or the 72 in the first innings at the Oval.

What the series did was firmly establish Flintoff as a national hero, and the world's No.1 all-rounder.

Kevin Pietersen

An Ashes series is not always the best place to make your Test debut, but Pietersen relished the challenge and three half-centuries in his first three innings appeared to show he was more than capable of living up to his potential.

But the best gauge of how good a player's temperament is comes when they are really under pressure, and the heat of the Test match arena is at boiling point. Pietersen certainly found out how hot it could get on the final day at the Oval and, although his technique – which had been scrutinised before the series had even started – did not always stand up to the examination, there was no doubting his determination.

He took a series of blows on the body from Brett Lee, but refused to be bowed in the face of the Australian onslaught as they homed in on an unlikely victory.

His 158 was typically aggressive and although he took risks in fighting back positively, it paid off. In the end, Australia had nothing left in the tank, and were forced to wait until the new ball arrived – and by then it was too late as victory had already slipped from their grasp.

Had it not been for that match-saving century, Pietersen's Ashes would have represented a promising start rather than a resounding success.

He left himself open to criticism by dropping a host of catches throughout the summer. But he deflected attention away from that with the way he approached his batting, which was a breath of fresh air.

It also relieved some of the pressure on Flintoff to produce the fireworks on a regular basis.

Shane Warne

The greatest spinner in the history of the game had his best series in England from a personal point of view, with 40 wickets at 19 runs apiece, but it meant nothing to him in the context of the result.

Warne entered this Ashes series touted as one of Australia's two main threats, but Glenn McGrath's impact was reduced significantly through a freak injury before the second Test at Edgbaston – thus heaping a huge responsibility on the leg-spinner.

He did not shy away from the challenge. In fact, he embraced it fully, and was still able to instill the jitters in the England batsmen even while holding up a misfiring attack.

Although he has restricted his repetoire of deliveries in recent years, Warne still managed to produce deliveries which almost defied the laws of geometry – including a stunning ball to take Andrew Strauss' wicket in the Second Test.

What was just as remarkable was the 35-year-old's willingness for a fight, highlighted by the marathon 31-over spell on the final afternoon at the Oval as he refused to give up a lost cause.

Warne also proved a doughty competitor with the bat, almost pulling off an unexpected victory at Edgbaston with 42 after the top order had been blown away.

It was not the last time he would prove a thorn in England's side with the willow, and few would have begrudged him a maiden Test match century in the draw at Old Trafford had he managed to get there. He finished the series to the sound and sight of some richly deserved standing ovations from the home fans.

Celebration time

The midday sun shone, England captain Vaughan paraded the world's most famous urn before thousands of fans shoehorned into Trafalgar Square, and for the first time in the summer 'Freddie' Flintoff (right) was not at his best.

The man who had done more than anyone to wrest cricket's greatest prize from the Aussie stranglehold was struggling to walk. In a straight line at least.

Then again, it was only a matter of hours since England had regained the Ashes and Flintoff had been celebrating for England in the manner in which he played. Extremely hard.

'I am struggling,' said Flintoff, who admitted to toasting the dawn with a gin and tonic.

'I've not been to bed yet. It's been an emotional roller-coaster, but it's fantastic. We came out on top and we're enjoying it.'

That could not have been more obvious as businessmen broke off work to watch from windows, parties struck up on roofs and those in the London Eye's highest pods were treated to a perfect view of the best show in town.

England's cricketers, of course, are not the first sports team to have taken a bow in an open-top bus around the streets of London.

Two years ago the World Cup-winning rugby stars were there. Last year it was the turn of Britain's Olympians. And they were all worthy.

Cricket followers in their tens of thousands turned out in London to applaud England on their Ashes triumph with (left from clockwise) Andrew Flintoff, Kevin Pietersen, Marcus Trescothick and, below, Michael Vaughan and his wife Nichola, revelling in the party atmosphere

But somehow this was different. This party, just 18 hours after the event, was an undiluted outpouring of the emotion which had kept the nation transfixed for the previous two months.

From the moment the bus appeared and the fans struck up a rendition of 'Ingerland, Ingerland, Ingerland' the atmosphere was as intoxicating as Freddie and Co's morning tipple. And all on a day when the burning sun bedecked London's famous landmark in its most brilliant hue.

'As they say, the sun shines on the righteous,' observed former England captain David Gower.

As the England heroes emerged – and let's not forget the Ashes-winning-women's side in the bus behind – Vaughan had his arms around the shoulders of coach Fletcher, who actually smiled.

Not one of those little mouth-curling ones for the cameras but the great beaming grin of a contented winner. Quite something for Fletcher.

The rest emerged in batting order, Trescothick, Strauss, Bell, etc, with the loudest cheers unsurprisingly reserved for Flintoff and, of course, the final match-winner Pietersen.

'KP for PM', proclaimed one banner, and how Tony Blair must wish he could capture the imagination of the general public with a fraction of the charismatic force of Pietersen's crucial 158.

Inevitably, for what must have been the hundredth time since the heady denouement of the day before, Vaughan was asked what it meant to be in possession of that urn.

'Cricket has captured the imagination of the nation, this is fantastic, beyond a dream,' said Vaughan.

'When England players win at any sport, the fans are the best in the world.'

Cue even more cheers and the arrival on stage of Victor Flowers, Barmy Army cheerleader and Jimmy Saville lookalike, wearing a huge hat and waving a flag of St George.

In normal circumstances, such an intrusion might see the offender ushered away by a pack of stewards but, in keeping with the party mood, Pietersen and Trescothick hugged him and even offered him Vaughan's seat.

It was just one more act to sum up the extraordinary warmth between players and supporters during this Ashes series.

Cornet player Billy Cooper, whose tune for each player was an integral part of the Test atmosphere, also piped up and the fervent hope was that just yards away down in Whitehall, ministers of a

Government which has not always kept its promises where sport is concerned were listening.

If the Ashes have proved anything, it is that sport has the power to lift the mood of a nation. Sport, in the manner cricket has been played these past two months, has the capacity to inspire values of respect, honour and camaraderie. It can make a difference.

Celebrities such as Rory Bremner, Stephen Fry and former umpire Dickie Bird, who added his approval to a series universally regarded as the best ever, all joined the party.

'I umpired three of the Tests in 1981 when Ian Botham was doing his stuff and this was better than all that,' insisted Bird. Swing-bowler Hoggard added: 'The country has gone cricketing mad and it's great for the game.'' Fellow paceman Jones, who went on to pay tribute to Vaughan as 'a great skipper', added: 'We've done them.'

After which Vaughan promptly lifted the Ashes urn once more to all corners of Trafalgar Square and the team joined in with renditions of 'Rule Britannia', 'Land of Hope and Glory', and the National Anthem.

Blatantly patriotic. Irresistibly uplifting.

And fittingly, it was all enacted under the statue of Admiral Horatio Nelson, whose last signal at the Battle of Trafalgar demanded: 'England expects every man to do his duty.'

No one could say England's cricketers had not done exactly that during a memorable sporting summer.

What they said

England captain Michael Vaughan: 'Finally we have our hands on the little urn. It's an amazing feeling. It's been a roller-coaster. It's been a hell of a summer of cricket, a hell of a Test series, but the players have produced some magnificent performances when it really mattered.

'You can talk about individuals, but the team effort and the management deserve huge credit.

'At the beginning of the summer it was a distant dream but they believe in their ability. It has been an extraordinary team effort and I am just the lucky one who picked up the urn.

'The response the public has given us throughout the whole summer means I am not too sure cricket will ever get to the same level again. I hope it does and I play in many more like this, but it is unlikely.

'It's something I would like to experience again but I'm not sure if we will – I'm not sure how this summer can be beaten.

'I'm sure my wife will say it's been a nightmare living with me for the last eight weeks – all I've thought about is beating Australia and how we're going to beat them. I'm sorry to the wife and family, but I've really focused on the huge job in hand.'

Andrew Flintoff: 'I'm going to have a stinking hangover. It's been a special few weeks. The family have had a strange few weeks, the profiles have been changed – we've been on the front page, the middle pages, the missus has been asked to do articles.

'They said when we won the Ashes it would be life-changing, and I think we've had a small taste of it. We've just got to enjoy it, for two weeks anyway.

'It's been an unbelievable day and I can't find the words to describe how KP [Kevin Pietersen] played. It's one of the great innings.

'He rode his luck, but the way he played under extreme pressure really epitomised what this side is about.

'But then we've all performed at different times. The strength of this side is that different people have stuck their hands up at different times during the series.

'It's been competitive out in the middle, but there has also been great respect between the two sides.'

Marcus Trescothick: 'It's been a long five years of hard work. We have put in the groundwork to give us the platform, we've kicked on in the last two years and this is the reward we deserved.

'It was a really special innings from KP, he was brilliant for us and it was just a great day.'

England coach Duncan Fletcher: 'It's taken a long time. You can start three or four years ago, there were players I was very excited about – it's probably come a bit early, but we're not complaining.

'It stems from a few years ago when we played Australia – there were tactics then, we play so often that you add little bits here and there. All the guys think they can still improve.'

Andrew Strauss: 'It's been seven weeks of emotional turmoil. I'm so proud to be part of this team.

'Everyone has contributed, every person – it makes you proud to represent your country. We've been on the edge of our nerves, but it's a great privilege to be here.'

Ashley Giles: 'I think all the wives help the guys along. You can see how they've supported us.

'Sorry to the headmistress of our kids' school because they weren't there for the last day of the series – but I think she'll understand.

'After the lows of Lord's, you would swap it for this. We knew we could do it but we had to play some good cricket after one bad Test.'

Kevin Pietersen: 'I would be stupid to say I have had a better day. That is the best innings I will ever play. With all the circumstances, it would be difficult to beat that.

'I've copped a bit of stick from a few people, but I do like a big stage. I knew I had to bat for a long time and managed to do it.

'Shane Warne dropped me, but then I've dropped six catches this series. I'll take the hundred.

'It is remarkable to be part of this England team. Everybody loves being in each other's company.

'The boys have been absolutely magnificent the whole two months we played. Every single bloke in the team is very special. The summer has been fantastic.'

Paul Collingwood: 'It was quite nerve-wracking. It's been a nail-biting series with some excellent games, but it's worse watching at home than playing in it. It's great for the boys that all of the hard work has come down to this.'

Australia captain Ricky Ponting: 'England fully deserved their result. The truth is they outplayed us for all four Tests after the first one.

'There are not too many regrets for us but we have not played our best cricket, mainly because England have not allowed us to.

'The chances were there for us, but we could not take them. But I would still rank England second. We are regarded No.1 in the world for what we have achieved over a long period of time.

'But I can't say I expect it to be a great reception for us when we arrive home. All the guys gave it their best shot, we have just not played well.

'But it's the best series I've been part of, and I'm looking forward to our next battle with England.

'Speculation about my future has already started, I cannot help that, people have their opinions. I don't feel obliged to reconsider my position.'

Shane Warne: 'I think we're still probably the best side in the world because we've done it over a period of time, both home and away, against every opposition and all the conditions that have been put up against us.

'But there's no reason England can't do that – if they play like they have through this series, they could be the best side in the world once they've played everybody home and away in a few years' time.

'I think England deserved to win and they outplayed us for the last four Test matches.

'We can say we should have done this and we should have done that, but at the end of the day I just think England deserved to win. We didn't really deserve to win.

'It's been a fantastic series and the spirit it was played in was brilliant. It's hard to say that when you lose because I don't like losing, but I've tried as hard as I can through the series and I'm pretty proud of myself the way that I've done.

'It's been my best-ever series, but unfortunately it's not been good enough. Anyone who has seen me play over the last 15 years will say I've given everything I've got, but you have to give credit to England.'

Adam Gilchrist: 'It's something different for this group of players. We've been No.1 in both forms of the game. We've held every trophy against every country at some stage along the way.

'Now the ultimate goal is the challenge to win it back, and we'll relish that. All things come to an end – our 18 years have been significant and we never gave up, we kept ourselves alive even when we weren't playing our best cricket.

'We kept it going until the last day of the series. Hopefully people will take heart from that.'

England's Series Stats...

Batting

	M	I	NO	Runs	HS	Avge	100	50	Ct	St
K.P.Pietersen	5	10	1	473	158	52.55	1	3	-	-
M.E.Trescothick	5	10	0	431	90	43.10	-	3	3	-
A.Flintoff	5	10	0	402	102	40.20	1	3	3	-
A.J.Strauss	5	10	0	393	129	39.30	2	-	6	-
S.P.Jones	4	6	4	66	20*	33.00	-	-	1	-
M.P.Vaughan	5	10	0	326	166	32.60	1	1	2	-
G.O.Jones	5	10	1	229	85	25.44	-	1	15	1
A.F.Giles	5	10	2	155	59	19.37	-	1	5	-
I.R.Bell	5	10	0	171	65	17.10	-	2	8	-
S.J.Harmison	5	8	2	60	20*	10.00	-	-	1	-
P.D.Collingwood	1	2	0	17	10	8.50	-	-	1	-
M.J.Hoggard	5	9	2	45	16	6.42	-	-	-	-

Bowling

	O	M	R	W	Avge	Best	5w	10w	SR
S.P.Jones	102	17	378	18	21.00	6-53	2	-	34.00
A.Flintoff	194	32	655	24	27.29	5-78	1	-	48.50
M.J.Hoggard	122.1	15	473	16	29.56	4-97	-	-	45.81
S.J.Harmison	161.1	22	549	17	32.29	5-43	1	-	56.88
A.F.Giles	160	18	578	10	57.80	3-78	-	-	96.00
P.D.Collingwood	4	0	17	0	-	-	-	-	-
I.R.Bell	7	2	20	0	-	-	-	-	-
M.P.Vaughan	5	0	21	0	-	-	-	-	-

Best Individual Scores

M.P.Vaughan	166	Old Trafford
K.P.Pietersen	158	The Oval
A.J.Strauss	129	The Oval
A.J.Strauss	106	Old Trafford
A.Flintoff	102	Trent Bridge
M.E.Trescothick	90	Edgbaston
G.O.Jones	85	Trent Bridge
A.Flintoff	73	Edgbaston
A.Flintoff	72	The Oval
K.P.Pietersen	71	Edgbaston

Best Innings Bowling

S.P.Jones	6/53	Old Trafford
S.J.Harmison	5/43	Lord's
S.P.Jones	5/44	Trent Bridge
A.Flintoff	5/78	The Oval
A.Flintoff	4/71	Old Trafford
A.Flintoff	4/79	Edgbaston
M.J.Hoggard	4/97	The Oval
A.Flintoff	3/52	Edgbaston
S.J.Harmison	3/54	Lord's
M.J.Hoggard	3/70	Trent Bridge

Leading run-scorers

	Runs	Matches
K.P.Pietersen	473	5
M.E.Trescothick	431	5
A.Flintoff	402	5
A.J.Strauss	393	5
M.P.Vaughan	326	5
G.O.Jones	229	5
I.R.Bell	171	5
A.F.Giles	155	5
S.P.Jones	66	4
S.J.Harmison	60	5

Best Match Bowling

S.J.Harmison	8/97	Lord's
S.P.Jones	7/110	Old Trafford
A.Flintoff	7/131	Edgbaston
S.P.Jones	5/59	Trent Bridge
A.Flintoff	5/78	The Oval
A.Flintoff	5/136	Old Trafford
M.J.Hoggard	5/142	Trent Bridge
A.F.Giles	5/146	Edgbaston
M.J.Hoggard	4/97	The Oval
S.J.Harmison	4/141	Trent Bridge

Team Totals

477	Trent Bridge
444	Old Trafford
407	Edgbaston
373	The Oval
335	The Oval
280 for 6d	Old Trafford
182	Edgbaston
180	Lord's
155	Lord's
129 for 7	Trent Bridge

How's that: Simon Jones' six for 53 at Old Trafford was the best of the series in a single innings for England

Most sixes

	Sixes	Matches
K.P.Pietersen	14	5
A.Flintoff	11	5
M.E.Trescothick	3	5
A.J.Strauss	2	5
G.O.Jones	2	5
S.P.Jones	1	4
M.P.Vaughan	1	5
S.J.Harmison	1	5
I.R.Bell	1	5

Most 50s and 100s

	50s	100s	Matches
A.Flintoff	4	1	5
K.P.Pietersen	4	1	5
M.E.Trescothick	3	-	5
M.P.Vaughan	2	1	5
A.J.Strauss	2	2	5
I.R.Bell	2	-	5
A.F.Giles	1	-	5
G.O.Jones	1	-	5

Leading duck-makers

	Ducks	Matches
S.J.Harmison	3	5
S.P.Jones	2	4
A.F.Giles	2	5
M.J.Hoggard	2	5
I.R.Bell	2	5
M.P.Vaughan	1	5
A.Flintoff	1	5
K.P.Pietersen	1	5

Most fours

	Fours	Matches
M.E.Trescothick	64	5
K.P.Pietersen	51	5
A.J.Strauss	50	5
A.Flintoff	49	5
M.P.Vaughan	45	5
G.O.Jones	29	5
A.F.Giles	17	5
I.R.Bell	17	5
S.P.Jones	10	4
S.J.Harmison	8	5

Five-wicket hauls

	Five wickets	Matches
S.P.Jones	2	4
A.Flintoff	1	5
S.J.Harmison	1	5

Wicketkeeper

	Dismissals	Stumpings	Matches
G.O.Jones	16	1	5

Leading catches
(excluding wicket-keeper)

	Catches	Matches
I.R.Bell	8	5
A.J.Strauss	6	5
A.F.Giles	5	5
M.E.Trescothick	3	5
A.Flintoff	3	5
M.P.Vaughan	2	5

Ton up: Opener Andrew Strauss hit two centuries against the Aussies

Australia's Series Stats...

Batting

	M	I	NO	Runs	HS	Avge	100	50	Ct	St
J.L.Langer	5	10	1	394	105	43.77	1	2	2	-
R.T.Ponting	5	9	0	359	156	39.88	1	1	4	-
M.J.Clarke	5	9	0	335	91	37.22	-	2	2	-
G.D.McGrath	3	5	4	36	20*	36.00	-	-	1	-
M.L.Hayden	5	10	0	318	138	35.33	1	-	10	-
S.K.Warne	5	9	0	249	90	27.66	-	1	5	
S.M.Katich	5	9	0	248	67	27.55	-	2	4	-
B.Lee	5	9	3	158	47	26.33	-	-	2	-
A.C.Gilchrist	5	9	1	181	49*	22.62	-	-	18	1
D.R.Martyn	5	9	0	178	65	19.77	-	1	4	-
M.S.Kasprowicz	2	4	0	44	20	11.00	-	-	3	-
S.W.Tait	2	3	2	8	4	8.00	-	-	-	-
J.N.Gillespie	3	6	0	47	26	7.83	-	-	1	-

Bowling

	O	M	R	W	Avge	Best	5w	10w	SR
R.T.Ponting	6	2	9	1	9.00	1-9	-	-	36.00
S.K.Warne	252.5	37	797	40	19.92	6-46	3	2	37.92
G.D.McGrath	134	22	440	19	23.15	5-53	2	-	42.31
B.Lee	191.1	25	822	20	41.10	4-82	-	-	57.35
S.W.Tait	48	5	210	5	42.00	3-97	-	-	57.60
S.M.Katich	12	1	50	1	50.00	1-36	-	-	72.00
M.S.Kasprowicz	52	6	250	4	62.50	3-80	-	-	78.00
J.N.Gillespie	67	6	300	3	100.00	2-91	-	-	134.00
M.J.Clarke	2	0	6	0	-	-	-	-	-

Best Individual Scores

R.T.Ponting	156	Old Trafford
M.L.Hayden	138	The Oval
J.L.Langer	105	The Oval
M.J.Clarke	91	Lord's
S.K.Warne	90	Old Trafford
J.L.Langer	82	Edgbaston
S.M.Katich	67	Lord's
D.R.Martyn	65	Lord's
R.T.Ponting	61	Edgbaston
J.L.Langer	61	Trent Bridge

Leading run-scorers

	Runs	Matches
J.L.Langer	394	5
R.T.Ponting	359	5
M.J.Clarke	335	5
M.L.Hayden	318	5
S.K.Warne	249	5
S.M.Katich	248	5
A.C.Gilchrist	181	5
D.R.Martyn	178	5
B.Lee	158	5
J.N.Gillespie	47	3

Team Totals

387	Trent Bridge
384	Lord's
371 for 9	Old Trafford
367	The Oval
308	Edgbaston
302	Old Trafford
279	Edgbaston
218	Trent Bridge
190	Lord's
4 for 0	The Oval

Fast improver:
Shaun Tait came
into the side and
took five wickets
at a cost of 42
runs apiece

Best Innings Bowling

S.K.Warne	6/46	Edgbaston
S.K.Warne	6/122	The Oval
S.K.Warne	6/124	The Oval
G.D.McGrath	5/53	Lord's
G.D.McGrath	5/115	Old Trafford
G.D.McGrath	4/29	Lord's
S.K.Warne	4/31	Trent Bridge
S.K.Warne	4/64	Lord's
B.Lee	4/82	Edgbaston
S.K.Warne	4/99	Old Trafford

Best Match Bowling

S.K.Warne	12/246	The Oval
S.K.Warne	10/162	Edgbaston
G.D.McGrath	9/82	Lord's
S.K.Warne	8/133	Trent Bridge
S.K.Warne	6/83	Lord's
B.Lee	5/105	Lord's
G.D.McGrath	5/157	The Oval
B.Lee	5/160	Old Trafford
B.Lee	5/193	Edgbaston
G.D.McGrath	5/201	Old Trafford

Most sixes

S.K.Warne	5	5
B.Lee	3	5
J.L.Langer	2	5
R.T.Ponting	2	5
J.N.Gillespie	1	3
M.L.Hayden	1	5
A.C.Gilchrist	1	5

Five-wicket hauls

	Five wickets	Matches
S.K.Warne	3	5
G.D.McGrath	2	3

Most 50s and 100s

	50s	100s	Matches
J.L.Langer	3	1	5
R.T.Ponting	2	1	5
S.M.Katich	2	-	5
M.J.Clarke	2	-	5
D.R.Martyn	1	-	5
M.L.Hayden	1	1	5
S.K.Warne	1	-	5

Wicketkeeper

	Dismissals	Stumpings	Matches
A.C.Gilchrist	19	1	5

Leading catches
(excluding wicket-keeper)

	Catches	Matches
M.L.Hayden	10	5
S.K.Warne	5	5
D.R.Martyn	4	5
R.T.Ponting	4	5
S.M.Katich	4	5
M.S.Kasprowicz	3	2
J.L.Langer	2	5
B.Lee	2	5
M.J.Clarke	2	5
G.D.McGrath	1	3

Most fours

	Fours	Matches
J.L.Langer	48	5
M.J.Clarke	48	5
M.L.Hayden	44	5
R.T.Ponting	39	5
S.K.Warne	32	5
S.M.Katich	32	5
D.R.Martyn	24	5
A.C.Gilchrist	24	5
B.Lee	19	5
G.D.McGrath	6	3

Leading duck-makers

	Ducks	Matches
J.N.Gillespie	2	3
S.K.Warne	2	5
M.S.Kasprowicz	1	2
G.D.McGrath	1	3
M.L.Hayden	1	5
R.T.Ponting	1	5

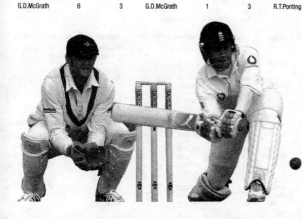

Glove story: Aussie wicketkeeper Adam Gilchrist, left, had a disappointing series

All-time records...

England Test Match Results v Australia

Played	Wins	Losses	Draws	Ties	NR
311	97	126	88	0	0

For England Against Australia
Best Individual Scores

L.Hutton	364	The Oval	1938
R.E.Foster	287	Sydney	1903/4
K.F.Barrington	256	Old Trafford	1964
W.R.Hammond	251	Sydney	1928/29
W.R.Hammond	240	Lord's	1938
W.R.Hammond	231*	Sydney	1936/37
E.Paynter	216*	Trent Bridge	1938
D.I.Gower	215	Edgbaston	1985
N.Hussain	207	Edgbaston	1997
W.R.Hammond	200	Melbourne	1928/29

For Australia Against England
Best Individual Scores

D.G.Bradman	334	Headingley	1930
R.B.Simpson	311	Old Trafford	1964
R.M.Cowper	307	Melbourne	1965/66
D.G.Bradman	304	Headingley	1934
D.G.Bradman	270	Melbourne	1936/37
W.H.Ponsford	266	The Oval	1934
D.G.Bradman	254	Lord's	1930
J.L.Langer	250	Melbourne	2002/3
D.G.Bradman	244	The Oval	1934
S.G.Barnes	234	Sydney	1946/47

Best Innings Bowling for England

J.C.Laker	10/53	Old Trafford	1956
J.C.Laker	9/37	Old Trafford	1956
G.A.Lohmann	8/35	Sydney	1886/87
H.Verity	8/43	Lord's	1934
R.G.D.Willis	8/43	Headingley	1981
G.A.Lohmann	8/58	Sydney	1891/92
W.Rhodes	8/68	Melbourne	1903/04
L.C.Braund	8/81	Melbourne	1903/04
T.Richardson	8/94	Sydney	1897/98
B.J.T.Bosanquet	8/107	Trent Bridge	1905

Best Innings Bowling for Australia

A.A.Mailey	9/121	Melbourne	1919/20
F.Laver	8/31	Old Trafford	1909
G.D.McGrath	8/38	Lord's	1997
A.E.Trott	8/43	Adelaide	1894/95
R.A.L.Massie	8/53	Lord's	1972
H.Trumble	8/65	The Oval	1902
S.K.Warne	8/71	Brisbane	1994/95
R.A.L.Massie	8/84	Lord's	1972
C.J.McDermott	8/97	Perth	1990/91
C.J.McDermott	8/141	Old Trafford	1985

Best Match Bowling for England

J.C.Laker	19/90	Old Trafford	1956
H.Verity	15/104	Lord's	1934
W.Rhodes	15/124	Melbourne	1903/04
A.V.Bedser	14/99	Trent Bridge	1953
W.Bates	14/102	Melbourne	1882/83
S.F.Barnes	13/163	Melbourne	1901/02
T.Richardson	13/244	Old Trafford	1896
J.C.White	13/256	Adelaide	1928/29
F.Martin	12/102	The Oval	1890
G.A.Lohmann	12/104	The Oval	1886

Best Match Bowling for Australia

R.A.L.Massie	16/137	Lord's	1972
F.R.Spofforth	14/90	The Oval	1882
M.A.Noble	13/77	Melbourne	1901/02
F.R.Spofforth	13/110	Melbourne	1878/79
B.A.Reid	13/148	Melbourne	1990/91
A.A.Mailey	13/236	Melbourne	1919/20
C.T.B.Turner	12/87	Sydney	1887/88
H.Trumble	12/89	The Oval	1896
S.C.G.MacGill	12/107	Sydney	1998/99
H.Trumble	12/173	The Oval	1902

England's Highest Totals

903 for 7d	The Oval	1938
658 for 8d	Trent Bridge	1938
636	Sydney	1928/29
627 for 9d	Old Trafford	1934
611	Old Trafford	1964
595 for 5d	Edgbaston	1985
592 for 8d	Perth	1986/87
589	Melbourne	1911/12
577	Sydney	1903/4
576	The Oval	1899

Australia's Highest Totals

729 for 6d	Lord's	1930
701	The Oval	1934
695	The Oval	1930
659 for 8d	Sydney	1946/47
656 for 8d	Old Trafford	1964
653 for 4d	Headingley	1993
645	Brisbane	1946/47
641 for 4d	The Oval	2001
632 for 4d	Lord's	1993
604	Melbourne	1936/37

Most matches for England

M.C.Cowdrey	43
G.A.Gooch	42
D.I.Gower	42
J.B.Hobbs	41
W.Rhodes	41
G.Boycott	38
I.T.Botham	36
A.C.MacLaren	35
R.G.D.Willis	35
A.P.E.Knott	34

England's Lowest Totals

45	Sydney	1886/87
52	The Oval	1948
53	Lord's	1888
61	Melbourne	1901/02
61	Melbourne	1903/04
62	Lord's	1888
65	Sydney	1894/95
72	Sydney	1894/95
75	Melbourne	1894/95
77	The Oval	1882

Australia's Lowest Totals

36	Edgbaston	1902
42	Sydney	1887/88
44	The Oval	1896
53	Lord's	1896
58	Brisbane	1936/37
60	Lord's	1888
63	The Oval	1882
65	The Oval	1912
66	Brisbane	1928/29
68	The Oval	1886

Most matches for Australia

S.E.Gregory	52
A.R.Border	47
S.R.Waugh	46
W.W.Armstrong	42
R.W.Marsh	42
C.Hill	41
V.T.Trumper	40
M.A.Noble	39
W.A.S.Oldfield	38
D.G.Bradman	37

England's Top Scorers

	Runs	Matches
J.B.Hobbs	3636	41
D.I.Gower	3269	42
G.Boycott	2945	38
W.R.Hammond	2852	33
H.Sutcliffe	2741	27
J.H.Edrich	2644	32
G.A.Gooch	2632	42
M.C.Cowdrey	2433	43
L.Hutton	2428	27
K.F.Barrington	2111	23

Australia's Top Scorers

	Runs	Matches
D.G.Bradman	5028	37
A.R.Border	3548	47
S.R.Waugh	3200	46
C.Hill	2660	41
G.S.Chappell	2619	35
M.A.Taylor	2496	33
R.N.Harvey	2416	37
V.T.Trumper	2263	40
D.C.Boon	2237	31
W.M.Lawry	2233	29

Most hundreds – England

	Hundreds	Matches
J.B.Hobbs	12	41
W.R.Hammond	9	33
D.I.Gower	9	42
H.Sutcliffe	8	27
M.Leyland	7	20
J.H.Edrich	7	32
G.Boycott	7	38
Hon.F.S.Jackson	5	20
K.F.Barrington	5	23
L.Hutton	5	27

Most hundreds – Australia

	Hundreds	Matches
D.G.Bradman	19	37
S.R.Waugh	10	46
G.S.Chappell	9	35
A.R.Morris	8	24
A.R.Border	8	47
M.J.Slater	7	20
W.M.Lawry	7	29
D.C.Boon	7	31
W.M.Woodfull	6	25
M.E.Waugh	6	29

England

Most fifties (including 100s)

	Fifties	Matches
J.B.Hobbs	27	41
H.Sutcliffe	24	27
G.Boycott	21	38
D.I.Gower	21	42
J.H.Edrich	20	32

Australia

Most fifties (including 100s)

	Fifties	Matches
D.G.Bradman	31	37
A.R.Border	29	47
S.R.Waugh	24	46
M.A.Taylor	21	33
G.S.Chappell	21	35

England's Wicket-Takers

	Wickets	Matches
I.T.Botham	148	36
R.G.D.Willis	128	35
W.Rhodes	109	41
S.F.Barnes	106	20
D.L.Underwood	105	29
A.V.Bedser	104	21
R.Peel	102	20
J.Briggs	97	31
T.Richardson	88	14
J.A.Snow	83	20

England: 5-wicket hauls

	Five wickets	Matches
S.F.Barnes	12	20
T.Richardson	11	14
I.T.Botham	9	36
A.V.Bedser	7	21
J.Briggs	7	31
R.G.D.Willis	7	35
R.Peel	6	20
M.W.Tate	6	20
W.Rhodes	6	41
W.H.Lockwood	5	12

England: 10-wicket hauls

	Ten wickets	Matches
T.Richardson	4	14
G.A.Lohmann	3	15
J.Briggs	3	31
J.C.Laker	2	15
R.Peel	2	20

Leading catches
(excluding wicketkeeper)

	Catches	Matches
I.T.Botham	57	36
W.R.Hammond	43	33
M.C.Cowdrey	40	43
W.G.Grace	39	22
L.C.Braund	37	20
A.W.Greig	37	21
F.E.Woolley	36	32
W.Rhodes	36	41
A.Shrewsbury	29	23
A.C.MacLaren	29	35

Wicketkeeper

	Stumpings	Matches
A.F.A.Lilley	19	32
T.G.Evans	12	31
A.P.E.Knott	8	34
E.F.S.Tylecote	5	6
R.C.Russell	5	9

	Dismissals	Matches
A.P.E.Knott	105	34
A.F.A.Lilley	84	32
A.J.Stewart	78	26
T.G.Evans	76	31
R.W.Taylor	57	17

Leading duck-makers

	Ducks	Matches
I.T.Botham	10	36
D.Gough	9	17
J.Briggs	9	31
A.F.A.Lilley	9	32
P.C.R.Tufnell	8	12

Australia's Wicket-Takers

	Wickets	Matches
S.K.Warne	172	31
D.K.Lillee	167	29
H.Trumble	141	31
G.D.McGrath	136	25
M.A.Noble	115	39
R.R.Lindwall	114	29
C.V.Grimmett	106	22
G.Giffen	103	31
W.J.O'Reilly	102	19
C.T.B.Turner	101	17

Australia: 5-wicket hauls

	Five wickets	Matches
C.T.B.Turner	11	17
T.M.Alderman	11	17
C.V.Grimmett	11	22
D.K.Lillee	11	29
S.K.Warne	10	31
G.D.McGrath	9	25
H.Trumble	9	31
M.A.Noble	9	39
C.J.McDermott	8	17
W.J.O'Reilly	8	19

Australia: 10-wicket hauls

	Ten wickets	Matches
F.R.Spofforth	4	18
D.K.Lillee	4	29
S.K.Warne	4	31
W.J.O'Reilly	3	19
H.Trumble	3	31

Leading catches
(excluding wicketkeeper)

	Catches	Matches
G.S.Chappell	61	35
A.R.Border	57	47
M.A.Taylor	46	33
H.Trumble	45	31
M.E.Waugh	43	29
W.W.Armstrong	37	42
R.Benaud	32	27
I.M.Chappell	31	30
R.B.Simpson	30	19
J.M.Gregory	30	21

Wicketkeeper

	Stumpings	Matches
W.A.S.Oldfield	31	38
J.M.Blackham	24	32
J.J.Kelly	16	32
H.Carter	15	20
I.A.Healy	12	33

	Dismissals	Matches
R.W.Marsh	148	42
I.A.Healy	135	33
W.A.S.Oldfield	90	38
A.T.W.Grout	76	22
A.C.Gilchrist	70	15

Leading duck-makers

	Ducks	Matches
S.E.Gregory	11	52
S.K.Warne	10	31
G.D.McGrath	9	25
J.V.Saunders	8	12
C.Hill	8	41

What next for England?

England's outstanding Ashes triumph has given them the confidence and self-belief to topple Australia as the dominant force in world cricket over the next few years.

The 2–1 series victory over Australia, although impressive, is merely a starting point and the mark of any truly great team is to continue scaling new heights.

Captain Vaughan and coach Fletcher will certainly not allow this England team to dine out on their solitary Ashes success for very long.

Their next big challenge is to triumph in Pakistan and India – an achievement Australia rated as one of their best during 10 years at the top.

Pakistan will be a test of their resilience while India, possessing the best batting line-up in the world, will be their toughest assignment in the hot and dusty conditions which are so alien to the touring England players.

Although the Ashes success is not enough to usurp Australia at the top of the ICC Championship rankings, they now have the highest rating of any side other than the Aussies since a new system was introduced in 1993.

But even a 3-0 series whitewash over Pakistan is unlikely to see them claim top spot – unless Australia lose their home series against the West Indies.

Even with the aura of invincibility that surrounded the Aussies now damaged, it is bordering on impossible for them to crash in such spectacular fashion on their own turf.

However, if England's dynamic side emerge unscathed from their tough winter schedule they can then set their sights on becoming the first side to win a series in Australia since West Indies in 1993.

Fletcher and Vaughan will already be thinking ahead to the Ashes reunion Down Under. Providing the personnel stay fit England, with a perfectly balanced attack, should still have the players capable of testing any side in any conditions.

Hoggard is an expert at exploiting swinging conditions, while Simon Jones and all-rounder Flintoff can utilise both conventional and reverse swing and they have outright hostility and pace in abundance in Durham bowler Harmison.

Left-arm spinner Giles, often the first player critics suggest should be dropped, also provides a steady mixture of control and turn when surfaces suit, as he has proved in the past at home and on the sub-continent. Giles demonstrated during in the Ashes series that he is capable of making a significant contribution with the bat – shown as he hit the winning runs in the Fourth Test, and by his 50 as England sealed a series win in the Fifth Test.

Add those components to an enviable batting line-up including the varied talents of Trescothick, Strauss, Flintoff and Pietersen – who made his Test debut in some style this summer – and there is no reason why England cannot become the dominant force.

By contrast, the ageing Australia team could well be in a period of transition by the time the Ashes are contested again.

Most of the squad who toured England were over 30 and the poor form of Gillespie and worries over the sustained fitness of pace spearhead McGrath suggest the mighty Aussie powerhouse is starting to lose its all-conquering dominance.

Concern has already been expressed in Australia about the lack of fast bowlers coming through to replace the likes of McGrath and Lee, but that is not an area which is restricted solely to the Aussies.

England's most obvious weakness is their lack of back-up seamers, and this was underlined in the final Test at the Oval.

Both Tremlett and Anderson were overlooked in favour off all-rounder Collingwood when the influential Simon Jones was ruled out through injury, there was simply no one to step up.

If the Ashes series illustrated anything about modern cricket it was that only outright pace will gain results – it is no longer good enough to bowl around 80–85 mph and expect results.

They also have to identify a spinner capable of challenging Giles; Gareth Batty has been tried in the past, but has shown little to indicate that he is the next man in waiting.

Wicketkeeping is also an area of concern after another error-strewn series from Geraint Jones, who fumbled chances with regularity.

He was picked largely for his batting skills, and the selectors will point to his impressive stand with Flintoff in the Fourth Test as justification of his inclusion in the Test side.

Jones – and England – have been fortunate most of his dropped catches have not been that expensive, but there will come a time when that will not be the case and the search will continue to find a wicketkeeper capable of batting like Jones but performing better behind the stumps.

These are problems, however, that nearly every other team in the world would love to have and with the World Cup in the Caribbean now less than two years away, England will be hoping to transfer the performances they have delivered on the Test stage into the one-day arena.

Should they do that and lift the World Cup for the first time, there will be no doubt whatsoever the quiet revolution inspired by Vaughan and Fletcher really has ended with England becoming the No.1 force in the world.